MR BURNS

Anne Washburn

MR BURNS

a post-electric play

OBERON BOOKS
LONDON

WWW.OBERONBOOKS.COM

First published in 2014 by Oberon Books Ltd
521 Caledonian Road, London N7 9RH
Tel: +44 (0) 20 7607 3637 / Fax: +44 (0) 20 7607 3629
e-mail: info@oberonbooks.com
www.oberonbooks.com

Reprinted with revisions in 2014 (twice), 2015

Anne Washburn is hereby identified as author of this play
in accordance with section 77 of the Copyright, Designs and
Patents Act 1988. The author has asserted her moral rights.

A catalogue record for this book is available from the British
Library.

PB ISBN: 978-1-78319-140-6
E ISBN: 978-1-78319-639-5

Cover design by nbstudio.co.uk

Printed, bound and converted
by CPI Group (UK) Ltd, Croydon, CR0 4YY.

Visit www.oberonbooks.com to read more about all our books
and to buy them. You will also find features, author interviews and
news of any author events, and you can sign up for e-newsletters
so that you're always first to hear about our new releases.

Mr Burns was performed at the Almeida Theatre, London on Thursday 5 June 2014, with the following cast in alphabetical appearance:

GIBSON	Demetri Goritsas
MATT	Adrian der Gregorian
MRS KRABAPPEL	Adey Grummet
JENNY	Justine Mitchell
QUINCY	Wunmi Mosaku
COLLEEN	Jenna Russell
MARIA	Annabel Scholey
SAM	Michael Shaeffer
MUSICIANS	Fiona Digney
	Michael Henry

Director	Robert Icke
Design	Tom Scutt
Composers	Orlando Gough
	and Michael Henry
Lighting Design	Philip Gladwell
Sound Design	Tom Gibbons
Choreographer	Ann Yee
Musical Directors	Orlando Gough
	and Michael Henry
Casting	Julia Horan CDG
Assistant Director	Whitney Mosery
Costume Supervisor	Jemima Penny
Design Assistant	Fly Davis
Company Stage Manager	Maris Sharp
Deputy Stage Manager	Amy Griffin
Assistant Stage Manager	Lucy Holland

ALMEIDA
THEATRE

A small room with an international reputation, the Almeida began life as a literary and scientific society – complete with library, lecture theatre and laboratory. From the very beginning, our building existed to investigate the world.

Today, we make bold new work that asks big questions: of plays, of theatre and how we live.

We bring together the most exciting artists to take risks; to provoke, inspire and surprise our audiences; to interrogate the present, dig up the past and imagine the future.

Whether new work or reinvigorated classic, whether in our theatre, on the road or online, the Almeida makes work to excite and entertain with extraordinary live art, every day.

Artistic Director **Rupert Goold**
Artistic Associate **Jenny Worton**
Associate Director **Robert Icke**

The cast of *American Psycho: A new musical thriller*
Photo: Manuel Harlan

Almeida Theatre, Almeida Street, London N1 1TA
Registered charity no. 282167

Discover almeida.co.uk | 020 7359 4404
Like ▌f▐ /almeidatheatre
Follow 🐦 @AlmeidaTheatre

Principal Partner

ASPEN

Supported using public funding by
**ARTS COUNCIL
ENGLAND**

This play is set in the very near future

Then 7 years after that

Then 75 years after *that*.

Notes on the Play

In 2008 I was commissioned by the Civilians, an investigative theater group based in NYC, to work on an idea I'd been wondering about for years: what would happen to a pop culture narrative pushed past the fall of civilization.

For a week that summer director Steve Cosson and I hunkered in a disused bank vault/free rehearsal space deep under Wall Street with Civilians actors Quincy Bernstine, Maria Dizzia, Gibson Frazier, Matt Maher, Jenny Morris, Sam Wright, and Colleen Werthmann.

We tasked them with remembering *Simpsons* episodes, and the dialogue around the remembering of the episode in the first act (and the small section of the episode rehearsed in the second act) is largely verbatim from those sessions.

It should be noted that the characters in this play bear at best a passing, and in many cases none whatsoever, resemblance to the actors initially involved in the project.

What It Looks Like: all illumination is from ostensibly non-electric sources.

The first act takes place by firelight, outdoors.

The second act takes place in an interior under a skylight in the afternoon.

The third act takes place after nightfall, in an interior stage, lit with non-electric instrumentation: candles and oil lamps, probably, or gas.

The third act finale does use a motley assortment of electrical instruments, a few traditional theatrical lighting instruments but maybe also other old jury rigged pieces of electrical lighting – Christmas tree lights, practicals, etc., adapted with care and cunning.

Costuming is an interesting question. In the first act people wear normal clothes but all Gibson's camping gear should look very new.

In the second act, clothing is looking a little worn, with a few newly made (sewn, knit) pieces.

In the third act everyone is 'costumed' to look like The Simpsons and should be wearing a combination of vintage pieces from the early 21st century, and new pieces adeptly made from cloth, which don't look quite right to our eyes.

Characters

In order of appearance:

MATT

JENNY

MARIA

SAM

COLLEEN

GIBSON

QUINCY

MRS KRABAPEL

Notes on Notation

Words or phrases in square brackets are
thought/implied, but not said.

Sentences which don't end in periods are
thoughts which have come to a close but not
been entirely concluded or dropped.

Every story ends on
a dark and raging river

The First Act

A warm night in early October.

End of season crickets.

Faintly, we can hear a stream.

Four people around a fire, on a mixed arrangement of indoor chairs, sports or lawn chairs and a fancy new couch.

A woman is huddled a slight distance away, in relation to the group around the fire but not part of it.

There might be a guitar case, leaning against a tree or a pack nearby.

MATT: It starts…the episode starts with Bart getting letters saying "I'm going to kill you Bart".

JENNY: …Right…'I'm going to kill you Bart'…because doesn't Lisa, doesn't she have a pen pal or something?

MARIA: oh

MATT: No, that's something – uh – yes – she has a pen pal and that's like a that's an other yes it starts with she has a pen

JENNY: She has a pen pal from someone in some Asian country

MATT: Yes like a repressed country or something and uh Bart is like uh thinks that's – is making fun of her

JENNY: Something like that and then *he* gets a letter

MATT: Right right he gets the letter and it says written in what appears to be blood like: I'm going to kill you Bart

JENNY: But that's not how it starts-starts it starts – they're on the couch, Bart and Lisa and they're

MATT: Oh

JENNY: They're watching TV, right?

MATT: That is right. Yes. They are watching

JENNY/MATT: *Itchy and Scratchy.*

MARIA: Oh…

JENNY: And it's…some *Itchy and Scratchy* episode

MARIA: Is that…that's the cartoon show they watch, right? It's

JENNY: It's incredibly violent.

MATT: It's shockingly violent. And they think it's hilarious.

MARIA: Because they always die, right? They always die –

JENNY: The cat always dies. The cat always gets it really violently

MARIA: Somebody always gets chopped up to bits

JENNY: That's the cat. Itchy. Or is it Scratchy? Wait –

MATT: Itchy is the cunning mouse who always kills Scratchy who is the cat. And Bart and Lisa always think it's completely hilarious, it's disturbing, it's awesome

MARIA: I think. Yeah. I think I saw that the first time I saw that I thought oh…that's going too far.

MATT: It's absolutely going too far. It's so brilliant.

JENNY: So I remember that they're watching the episode and something…

MATT: They're watching it – and it's incredibly violent – and Lisa is totally cracking up and Bart *isn't*

JENNY: Yes yes yes that's right, right? And Lisa is saying, like, that's really funny Bart why aren't you laughing or something and Bart is full of gloom because he's depressed because someone is trying to kill him…

MATT: And then the doorbell rings and it's the mail

JENNY: *Yes.* And *that's* when Lisa gets the pen-pal letter

MATT: And Bart, yes, that's when Bart gets another death threat and like no one, like everyone's really blasé about it and at one point he's like – and everything is shot like *Cape Fear* so like there are like all these smash cuts where its just like: Dunnnnnngh – where like they start on a start on a shot and then sort of widen out in this way that *Cape Fear* like

MARIA: The second *Cape Fear*

MATT: The second the DeNiro so it's like it'll be he'll open a letter and suddenly it'll be like a smash cut on a letter like "I'm going to kill you Bart!" Oiiiiing! and then like widen out and at one point he's got all of the letters on the kitchen table and it's an overhead shot, all of these letters written in blood and it's like whomp whomp – well yeah that's the sound from the *Cape Fear* soundtrack that's the – whomp whomp whomp

JENNY: Oh, *yeah*: whomp whomp whomp whomp…

MATT/MARIA/JENNY: Whomp whomp whomp –

JENNY/MATT: Whomp

MARIA: *(Simultaneously.)* Wom – no.

JENNY/MATT/MARIA: whomp whomp whomp whomp, whomp whomp whomp whomp

> *MATT does a little conductoristic 'it goes here' gesture*

wom wom wom –

MATT: And so it's that, it's that and it's all of them sitting around the kitchen table and it's like 'die Bart die I'm going to kill you Bart dah dah dah dah dah' and then's like one written in pen and he's like this one is written in pen and Homer's like oh I wrote that one because when *(Laughs tumultuously.)* when when ah Bart 'oh I wrote that one because for that time when Bart tattooed this on my butt' and he like pulls down his pants and his butt is tattooed with the word 'wide load'

> *Laughter.*

and the whole family is like 'ahhhh!' and starts laughing laughing for like a really weirdly long time, Marge, Lisa, and the baby are just like: ha ha ha ha ha…it's very…I just thought it was funny that they would just take a break from the episode to laugh at Homer, anyway…

JENNY: There's a court case

MATT: Right. Right right right: the court case. But *before* the court case. At the end of that sequence. You see uh a

15

ketchup bottle spurting 'die Bart die' onto a letter it's a reveal and it's Sideshow Bob

MARIA: Sideshow Bob?

JENNY: Right played by Kelsey Grammer

MATT: And then he's like – yeah, played by Kelsey Grammer and then he's like:

MARIA: Not Mr. Burns?

MATT: No.

JENNY: No, it's Sideshow Bob.

MARIA: There isn't a fish. With three eyeballs.

MATT: Blinky. No. That's from the episode where Burns' nuclear power plant is polluting the Springfield river, and Bart tries to shut it down. But Burns doesn't actually try to kill him in that episode.

He *does* try to kill him *(Starts to laugh.)* he does try to kill him, multiple times, in 'Curse of the Flying Hellfish'.

MARIA: "Ex-cellent", right?

She flutters her fingers uncertainly.

MATT: *"Ex-cellent"*

He tents his expertly.

JENNY: And so he's writing letters. Sideshow Bob is writing letters. In ketchup.

MATT: And then he tastes the ketchup right before we go to a commercial – evily

(Tasting it.)

Mhhhhh

And then…

JENNY: And then he's on the stand.

MATT: Well there's a brief montage of him working out I remember there's a montage of him doing – all these menacing shots of him lifting weights and then aerobic calisthenics *(Mincing sprightly voice.)* "one and two and three and…" and that's that's when we see the tattoos

JENNY: Wait what are the tattoos?

MATT: There are, there are some tattoos 'cause you see shots of him in prison doing um oh yeah because he only has three fingers, because the Simpsons characters only have three fingers

JENNY: Wait, is it really only three?

MARIA: Yeah that seems

MATT: Plus thumbs.

MARIA: Oh…okay.

JENNY: That's so weird I didn't know that. But that's ignorance for you right.

MATT: So because he only has three fingers you see the tattoos and they say:

L-u-v and h – like…

JENNY: Oh that's from the um

MATT: From

JENNY: From Do The Right Thing

MATT: No no it's from Do The Right Thing is also stealing from…

SAM: Night /of the Hunter.

MATT: Night of the Hunter

JENNY: Oh

MATT: Night of the Hunter he has, the villain has love and hate

JENNY: Oh

MATT: Tattooed on his hand

SAM: Who's also Robert Mitchum

MATT: Who's also Robert Mitchum who plays *Cape Fear* who plays De Niro's character in the original *Cape Fear*

SAM: "There's only two things in this world, love, and hate"

MATT: Yeah well Sideshow Bob has love and hate but it's l-u-v with an umlaut and I don't know how they do hate but it's some weird they do some weird phonetic thing with the 'a' to make it read love and hate.

JENNY: And then we go right in after you see after that montage then you see it's Sideshow Bob in court

MATT: Yes

JENNY: And he's charming everyone in court…oh and doesn't he, doesn't Sideshow Bob have die Bart die tattooed on his chest and isn't she there a lady who's like, isn't she like: you have die Bart die and he's like no, that's German it says die Bart die

MATT: Die Bart die

> *COLLEEN laughs.*
>
> *Everyone turns towards her.*
>
> *She shrinks into herself again.*
>
> *They continue as if they were not now trying to engage her attention.*

MATT: And then woman the woman in the jury box says anyone who knows German can't be a can't

JENNY: Oh that's right: anyone who knows German –

MATT: Anyone who knows German has to be a very nice man

> *Laughter.*

JENNY: Anyone who speaks German, right

MATT: Anyone who speaks German

MARIA: Couldn't be

MATT: Couldn't be a bad man

> *Laughter.*

JENNY: The Bart the. It's so awesome.

MATT: And then the prosecutor – that's a common Simpsons character the smarmy like prosecutor "what are your feelings about Bart Simpson?"

MARIA: *(She doesn't.)* Oh that guy right I think I remember that guy

MATT: Aaaaaah, is it not true that you repeatedly threatened to kill Bart Simpson

"Bart Simpson, that spirited little scamp – and then you know all the lighting gets dark – *who twice foiled my evil schemes and sent me to this urine-soaked hell-hole…*" "we take exception to urine-soaked hell hole – we prefer pee-soaked stink hole" and Sideshow Bob is like "cheerfully withdrawn"

> *Laughter.*

SAM: *(More of a whisper.)* Heyhey –

> *His head is turned, looking into the woods around them.*
>
> *They stop. Everyone is alert, listening acutely. COLLEEN is frozen, listening.*
>
> *There is a very long pause.*

SAM: It's nothing. It's nothing. I thought I heard something.

> *He quotes, but does not do the voice:*

"Bart Simpson, that spirited little scamp"

MATT: Um… Right. Yes.

SAM: "Hellhole"

MATT: *(Super distracted.)* Right. And then – right. Yes, so that's that's pretty much it and then so he's free. After that.

JENNY: *(Ditto.)* Sideshow Bob is free. And he's walking…

MATT: and uh…

JENNY: And then it's him walking out of the courtroom.

MATT: *(Making a conscious effort to rally.)* It's him walking out of the courtroom. Yes. And there's a big shot of like, like 'woosh' there's a big shot of like, 'Paroled' across…

JENNY: And he's just, he's walking towards the camera looking at the camera until it's like right up against him.

MATT: So he has parole and they find out and *(Ah ha it comes to him.)* the Simpsons find out because they go to the movies and and it's again a spoof of a scene in *Cape Fear* like they all go to the movies and De Niro is sitting in front of them with a cigar

MARIA: Mh hm

MATT: Smoking a cigar and like laughing, Sideshow Bob is sitting in front of them like going: hah hah

MARIA: The only thing I can remember about that whole movie Juliet Lewis like sucks Robert De Niro's fingers in a gross way and then he bit Ileana Douglas' face, right?

JENNY: Right.

MARIA: Bit Ileana Douglas' face off that's all I remember.

JENNY: No no he kills the dog. Does he bite the lady's face?

MATT: He bites her face hard. But in front of Sideshow Bob, Homer is sitting with like an even bigger cigar laughing and laughing even louder and going "Hoh!" and Sideshow Bob is like "oh now really that's just inappropriate" and that's and Bart and uh Bart says uh: "it's you you're threatening to kill me!"

And Sideshow Bob says...... What does he say do you remember what he says what the dialogue is?

MARIA: ...no.

MATT: "It's you!" Bart says "you're the one who keeps sending me threatening letters," um...and Sideshow Bob says...

> *MATT laughs.*

oh god wait a minute – uh – uh there's some I remember I remember it's like...there's some, *thing,* where Sideshow Bob keeps meaning to say something dreadful but he says it's some linguistic thing where he says it wrong "*I'm –* " – oh, god it's really hard to

JENNY: That sounds totally familiar

MATT: they say something along the lines of "You...stay away from our son!" and Sideshow Bob retorts like "I..." oh this is torture I know this is really funny...

There's a blankish sort of pause.

MATT: Oh!

MARIA: Oh did you get it?

MATT: No. No but I just remembered well the whole first act is – who's sending letters so at one point Lisa is like: I know who did it and she calls up Moe the Bartender because she figures it must be Moe taking revenge for all the prank calls that Bart has been making and she calls the bar and Moe answers 'Moe's Tavern', and she's like Moe, we know its you and cut it out and Moe's like, "oh my goodness, alright", and he goes in the back and there's an enormous like crowd of pandas all hanging hiding out in the back because he's been smuggling pandas from China they're all playing poker at these little tables and he's like: *(Voice.)* "Okay guys the gig's up get out of here andele andele" and all these pandas run out of Moe's bar, like, trailing poker chips…

JENNY: Oh right. Right.

MARIA: And isn't there something where –

SAM: *(A driving whisper.)* Sssssssst.

> *SAM's hand is raised. His head is cocked. They all immediately fall silent, listening and watching him intently.*
>
> *They listen.*
>
> *SAM reaches behind him and pulls out a rifle. MATT pulls out a revolver and beams the flashlight through the forest offstage. MARIA and JENNY have pulled out revolvers; MARIA has a more powerful flashlight which she also runs through the darkness. JENNY has also pulled out a bowie knife and is placing it on the ground near her.*
>
> *COLLEEN is up and on her haunches. Absolutely taut, moving not a muscle. Eyes wild, flicking everywhere.*
>
> *MATT whispers: 'deer' and SAM shakes his head.*
>
> *They're all frozen, listening, only the light is moving.*
>
> *They hear something tiny, and all turn towards one direction.*
>
> *MATT and MARIA both turn their flashlights in the same spot.*

SAM stands and aims his revolver, MATT stands, still holding the flashlight, revolver out, JENNY is up and aiming, MARIA stays seated, her fingers gripped on the light.

COLLEEN fades into the trees, in the opposite direction.

SAM: Come out!

GIBSON: I'm alright!

SAM: Come out!

GIBSON: I'm alright!

SAM: Get out here!

Sound of footfalls in underbrush.

GIBSON: My name is Gibson, I'm on the road from –

GIBSON appears onstage, hands raised. He has a well-worn backpack and new-looking hiking boots, a new-looking windbreaker.

SAM stays standing with the rifle.

SAM: *(Not unkindly.)* Shut up.

MATT moves forward and slowly pats GIBSON down, removing his pack and handing it to JENNY.

JENNY goes through it slowly while MARIA, standing now, also covers GIBSON with her revolver and flashlight.

MATT immediately finds and removes a pistol from the inside of GIBSON's windbreaker. He continues to pat him down.

JENNY removes a knife kit almost immediately, and a very new atlas of the United States – which she sets aside – then packets of camping food, a portable water purifier, several rolls of toilet paper, clothes, and at the bottom a few books and journals. She replaces everything in order retaining only the knives and the atlas.

She picks up the atlas and looks through it, turning the pages carefully.

JENNY: Hey

SAM whistles, and looks through it briefly.

MATT: How much?

SAM: The whole country.

> *MATT comes over to look while retaining a loose gun trained on GIBSON, MARIA also still holds a gun on him.*
>
> *Together, silently, they find where they are and look carefully at the adjacent area.*
>
> *GIBSON is watching them with acute interest and manfully disguised anxiety.*
>
> *There is a moment, and then, with a lingering near-reluctance, it is returned to him.*
>
> *JENNY passes the pack back to MATT who passes it back to GIBSON although he retains the pistol.*
>
> *GIBSON stows the atlas back in the pack.*

MATT: Thank you.

Where are you coming from?

GIBSON: Framingham.

MATT: Framingham, that's…

GIBSON: Massachusetts.

JENNY: What part of the state?

MATT: It's near Holliston right?

GIBSON: Yeah, nearish. It's in the Eastern part of the state, near I-90.

SAM: How did you come down?

GIBSON: I took – well I went over to Boston first.

SAM/JENNY: How is Boston?

GIBSON: Boston is a mess.

JENNY: How bad is it?

GIBSON: Yeah.

It's really bad.

JENNY: I have a sister.

GIBSON: I didn't see any women, I'm sorry. I just. I got there, I got out of there.

SAM: And then which way.

GIBSON: I went down 24 to Brockton. I was hearing rumors about a barricade around Bridgewater so I cut over to 95 and took that down to Providence. Providence was deserted, weirdly, not even a lot of bodies, maybe there was some kind of evacuation? I don't know.

MARIA: I think they were hit early. So maybe the government cleared people out.

GIBSON: Maybe. I guess. It was eerie, I got out of there in a hurry, I thought I should head for Stamford, I skirted up –

MATT: My wife was in Stamford. On business. She'd just checked herself into the hospital there when the city was put under quarantine.

GIBSON: I didn't actually go into Stamford, it was burned through, but there were definitely people in the area and it seemed okay.

MATT: Yea high. Fair haired

SAM: Wait wait, let's do this let's do this properly okay. I think it's important to do this properly.

MARIA: Right

MATT: Right. Okay right.

> *They all take a moment to locate notebooks; SAM pulls a little spiral bound out of his short pocket, GIBSON digs into his pack, pulls out a school composition notebook with pages paperclipped towards the back.*

(To MARIA.) Do you want to start?

MARIA: Don't you?

MATT: No I'd rather. Uh. Give it a minute. You go.

MARIA: Mkay. Alright:

H. Harrison. Maureen Harrison. Don Harrison. 64, 65.

> *Microbeat – meaning GIBSON's notebook.*

You're not going to open that?

GIBSON: I've got a really good memory.

Microbeat of Maria Doubt.

Trust me. I really do.

MARIA: Holmes. Mel Holmes – that's a woman. 38.

K. Tim Kapner, Lisa Kapner

And they have two sons: Paul, he's 5. And Noah, 7.

Is it alright if I just look?

GIBSON: Yeah.

> *He hands the notebook over, she turns to the paperclipped section, scans a page, turns over scans another page, flips forward a few pages, looks, hands it back.*

MARIA: Okay. Thank you. I just had to, you know.

GIBSON: Of course.

MARIA: Um… L. Nilia Larkin 14

W. Miriam Westabrook 36

and then this is kind of crazy because she was in California.

SAM: That's not crazy. People got out of California.

MARIA: It's crazy but she's my best friend since college.

Celia Campinelli.

GIBSON: Yeah. No. I'm sorry.

MATT: *(To JENNY.)* Do you want to?

JENNY: You can. Go ahead.

MATT: D. DePaul.

Elizabeth DePaul 32

Cameron DePaul 38

E. Arden Edwards 22

I. Ingrassia. Lou Ingrassia, 39.

Jack Ingrassia 12

Stewart Ingrassia 6

Tabby Ingrassia 8 months.

L. Sarah Lewis 39.

(Tiny pause to see if that one landed.)

Erik Shanker 40

Timothy Wald 42

GIBSON, who has been listening acutely, looks up.

GIBSON: No. Sorry.

MATT: Yup. Jenny?

JENNY: Mkay.

She concentrates for a moment:

B. Butler.

Angela Butler, 71

Sharon Butler 46. This is Boston.

Richard Butler 52

C. Cohen.

Miriele Cohen 17

Nina Cohen 19

Raul Cohen 15

G. Garber. Mark Garber 37

Casey Martin 39

Rolo Martinez 50

GIBSON: Wait a minute. Casey Martin.

JENNY: Casey Martin?

GIBSON: I've got a Casey Martin.

JENNY: He's got brown hair almost 6 feet

GIBSON: Brown hair, tall, yes.

He's looking in the book, flipping pages a bit.

JENNY: Glasses

GIBSON: *(From memory, still finding the exact spot.)* Yes glasses

JENNY: Glasses and um,

She gestures around her own face, increasingly excited.

brown eyes?!

GIBSON: Glasses I don't know about the eyes.

JENNY: Lean. He's got a lean build.

GIBSON: Uh huh.

> *GIBSON finds the page.*

Bethesda.

JENNY: He's in Bethesda?

GIBSON: No, he's from Bethesda. Before that briefly D.C. and Scranton for college and before that Belmont. A "tiny tiny town in Maine".

JENNY: Oh. Fuck.

Okay.

Okay, that's not him.

GIBSON: He was working for Johns Hopkins Hospital in records administration.

JENNY: Yeah that's, that's really not him.

GIBSON: Sorry.

JENNY: I haven't talked to the guy in over a year, anyway, I don't even know why he's on my list. Um…

Do I have more?

> *She might be near tears at this point.*

That was my

That was my ten right? Or do I…

MATT: *(Gently.)* I wasn't counting it

GIBSON: I can do more.

> *She counts off swiftly on her fingers.*

JENNY: Oh, no. I have one more. Charlie Barnard.

> *She sort of throws her hands up.*

69. My crazy uncle. Shlumpy. Weird. I know you don't have him.

A pause.

GIBSON: No. Sorry.

JENNY: Sam?

SAM: H. Linda Hopkins 52

　S. Ginny – or Virginia – Scott 60

　　He stops, GIBSON waits for more.

GIBSON: That's it?

SAM: I come from a small town. I know about everybody else.

　　GIBSON nods.

JENNY: Oh, and we're also looking

　　She looks at MARIA and they both glance into the forest.

MARIA: We're also looking for a:

　　(In a carrying voice.)

　Becca Wright. 12.

　　(Low.)

　You don't have her.

GIBSON: *(His eyes flick into the forest.)* Oh…no.

MARIA: *(Low.)* I know.

　　(Loud.)

　Thank you.

GIBSON: *(Not a real question.)* Alright, so you're doing 10?

　　Everyone scrambles to get their notebooks open.

MARIA: Isn't it 10?

GIBSON: Seems like, last week or so, people are knocking it back to 8. Mine are:

　E. Evans. Peter Evans 70

　Estelle Evans 48

　Richard Kahn 35. Sorry, that's K. Kahn. Richard.

　L Jon Llewellyn. 37

S. Nolan Scott 36

MARIA: Okay wait, wait just a second

> *She's peering at her book and rotating it back and forth as she looks at names scribbled in the margins.*

Let me just – I've got to write out a new book. I didn't leave enough room for the S's.

Okay, no.

GIBSON: Suarez. Lilia Suarez 38.

Petra Suarez-Evans 2

Cynthia Warner 52

Francis Warner 22

Noah Warner 27

> *They flip back and forth in their notebooks.*

MATT: No. Sorry.

JENNY: No. Sorry.

MARIA: *(Shaking her head.)* Uh uh.

> *SAM is checking very methodically.*

SAM: No. I'm sorry.

> *A slight pause.*

MATT: Hungry?

GIBSON: No, I'm alright.

SAM: Beer?

GIBSON: *Yes.* That would be great. Thanks.

SAM: I'll get it.

> *He steps offstage into the shrubbery.*
>
> *There is another pause.*

MARIA: How long have you been moving?

GIBSON: About a, month and a half. I've been stopping here and, uh, stopping there. Mainly I've just been going.

> *Little beat.*

What about you?

JENNY: I've been here for about week. I'm from Baltimore. I left eleven weeks ago. I was in Wilmington for a while 'til about a month ago and then, I was really on the move for just about three weeks.

MATT: I got here four days ago. I was in New York. Then at my mother-in-law's cabin in the Catskills. I had to get out of there two weeks ago.

MARIA: I live here. Or, I lived here. Or no, I live here. Right, *(She gestures with deliberate vagueness.)* over there.

> *SAM returns with moist beers.*

SAM: Stream cooled.

GIBSON: Oooh nice. Nice. Thank you.

SAM: Pleasure.

> *SAM passes them around. GIBSON twists his beer open. They all sit down.*

You came down to Stamford on 95.

GIBSON: No I cut over to 84 after Richmond –

you heard that the Millstone plant went up too?

MATT: Millstone? What's that is that…

GIBSON: Nuclear, yeah, at Waterford.

MARIA: Where is that.

GIBSON: On the coast, near Mystic.

MARIA: Wait I don't know where – I just know the movie title that's –

GIBSON: Northeast corner, right near the border with Rhode Island.

MARIA: So that's – uh uh – how many miles from here?

GIBSON: Well well over a hundred fifty/ it's –

JENNY: So that's fine right?

GIBSON: 170-something. 177? 78? I can check my atlas.

JENNY: You weren't there.

GIBSON: No, no. I met a couple groups coming from there.

JENNY: They were there when it went up?

GIBSON: They were just scared. They were 20 miles away when it happened but they ran into some people coming from the area who were in rough shape.

JENNY: But that's fine.

MATT: It depends on the weather. On the wind.

JENNY: No but over one fifty?

MATT: I heard 10. I heard 20. I heard 50. I heard 50 miles but only for a few days. I heard 50 miles but only for a few months. I heard a hundred, for a hundred million years. I mean.

I just stay away. When I know how to stay away.

GIBSON: *(Looking at atlas.)* 186.

MATT: Waterford we're fine. There are other plants lots closer.

Well, there are.

SAM: *(Steering it away.)* Then you cut over to 84.

GIBSON: I cut over to 84; there are barricades on 84 from just east of Hartford until I don't know, I cut the whole scene a really wide berth, but I rejoined 84 just past Southington and it was fine. I crossed the river near Tarrytown.

MARIA: I heard that West Pennsylvania, that all of West Pennsylvania is…

JENNY: I don't think that's true. I think that's just a crazy rumor. I do.

SAM: There are a lot of crazy rumors.

JENNY: It's not like it was sudden. There were weeks and weeks and weeks where it was pretty clear – they had weeks and weeks and weeks to plan for this.

MATT: I think there was a lot of pressure, though. To keep the plants going, to keep the grid up, they were so worried about the grid going down and everyone freaking.

GIBSON: On the news there was this one guy who was saying, they no longer have the personnel, in a lot of places, that you can't just shut them down and walk away you have to have all of these people, hundreds of trained people, meticulously stow the uh, material away and uh, that they may have waited too long.

JENNY: I didn't see this. When was this.

GIBSON: It was local. It was one of the last broadcasts before everyone started to go off the air.

MATT: People are not competent. Can I just say that? People, are not competent.

There is a pause.

MARIA: I ran into a guy in the Wal Mart. We were talking about duct tape – there isn't any left at the Wal Mart, of course, and I never got any before because I thought, well, really, what's the use, and now I'm sorry because it's handy and I hate going into houses, I'm not good with the stink, so we were talking about where would still have it – he had a really good suggestion which is the janitorial areas at schools – and anyway we were talking about duct tape, and he had a cousin who worked at a nuclear power plant, Oyster Creek it's near Asbury Park and he said

JENNY: Where is that. Where is Asbury Park. How many miles from here.

GIBSON is reaching for his atlas.

MATT: It's around a hundred.

JENNY: A hundred.

MATT: Indian Point is actually a lot closer.

JENNY: How much closer.

MARIA: About 30.

There is a pause.

SAM: What did he say? The guy. You ran into him at the Wal Mart and he said.

MARIA: He said that they're that what happens is that when the plant operators take the plant offline that the cooling pools, which is where, you know

MATT: Right.

MARIA: That that whole system continues to operate and that the radioactivity, the rods, are fine, basically, for as long as there's electrical power to the plant. They just sit there, it's fine. And that when the power goes out there are massive generators, and they continue to power the plant and the cooling pools for, weeks. But then they run out of fuel.

And the electricity stopped, and the fires started and everyone is really, distracted, and he realizes, he gradually realizes, you know I don't think anyone *is* thinking about this. And the weeks are kind of…ticking away.

JENNY: The fires were before.

MATT: The fires. No. The fires were after.

JENNY: The fires started before the grid went down.

MATT: The big fires. The crazy explosions. Those were after.

JENNY: Not where I was.

SAM: It depended on where you were.

MATT: Babe.

JENNY: Yeah I'm just. All right. Before. After. Before. *(To MARIA.)* I'm sorry, he realizes.

He realizes no one is thinking about it.

MARIA: He uh…yeah.

There's a small pause.

He's thinking about it.

So he decides, well, okay. It's on me.

So he formulates this plan, where he's going to stock up on fuel and he's going to go to the plant, and find the generator shed, and he says the shed is going to be locked, because when people are panicking they aren't thinking they just lock. I'm going to have to break it open. I'll bring a crowbar I'll pry the fuck out of it I'll. I'll bust the shed open, and I'll refuel the generators, and that's, that's what I'll do, right, for months, that will be my task, this is what I will dedicate myself to, to refueling those massive generators. Until finally the generators will break down, because things always break down, but at that point…

I guess that that point it's different? The radioactivity has… settled? Or, like, the worst of it has bubbled away? He was excited, it wasn't clear.

MATT: It's still radioactive. It's still just as radioactive. For, like, a hundred thousand years it's still, just as radioactive.

MARIA: Yes but I think he thought it would be, the gasses wouldn't build up or whatever there wouldn't be this issue of explosions or plumes, anyway

JENNY: But he knew what he was talking about, right? He knew.

MARIA: Yeah but did he? His cousin worked in the guardbox at the gate. I mean, he had these terms.

And what he told me – in the power tool section – the ex-power tool section – at the Wal Mart in the saws aisle and the hilarious thing is that it's stripped absolutely clean – what he told me, was that he had gone to do it, he had, he was living fifteen miles away so he sets out he walks it it takes him a day and a half because of a – anyway he walks it and he's there, he's at a gas station a mile from the main entrance. It's an utterly gorgeous day and he's siphoning off one of the tanks. He has containers. He has a dolly, or – what are those things, where it's a couple of planks, basically, on wheels like this *(She indicates dimension.)* and usually it has strips of carpeting on it?

SAM: *(Helpfully.)* Yeah that's a dolly.

MARIA: Okay yes, so he has a dolly. He's got containers of gasoline. He's determined, he's set and ready to go. And then he has a, a. A flash? A very vivid – just like how you picture something, a waking fantasy.

And he can see himself, at the front gate of the plant. And there's reactor A, right above him.

And he doesn't look at it he presses on and up the little service roadway and he's at the shed, the the service shed and so he, yes, he's totally picturing himself busting at the lock, until he busts it open. And he this shed is vast, and shadowy, and at the end of it this hulking generator. And he's maneuvering the dolly inside when he realizes, that there's no noise, in the shed, these big machines and it's so quiet. He lowers the dolly. He steps inside. He walks, all the way across, boots on concrete. He reaches the silent generator and he touches it: it's cold, dead. He's too late.

And his heart is pounding. And he has a flutter in his stomach which he thought what is this, is this adrenaline? And he thinks: probably not. And this ache, starting up in his head.

JENNY: Wait this is how you know? Is that the first? Headache?

MARIA: This is what he. This is just what he said. He's got an ache. And the stomach.

And he leaves the shed and the reactor is right there, right above him, half lit up by sunlight, half in shadow.

And now he gets the first wave of nausea and. He discovers he's shitting his pants.

And.

This is weird.

He doesn't want the reactor to get to watch him die.

So he starts off, back down the road. And he's thinking, all I want is to get around that curve up there. So I'm out of sight. Feets, just carry me that far. Feets don't fail me now.

And this is the point where he snaps out of it. He's standing at the station, with his dolly, and, 6 gas canisters he's scrounged from garages, and a few plastic tubs he found in restaurants. Half of them full of gas. And he looks up the roadway leading to the plant. And he knows he can't do it. He drops the siphon. He walks away.

He said: it's not knowing, that's the problem.

He said: I think I can handle anything, if I know what it is

I just can't manage the dread.

> *Bitty pause.*

And then we talked about duct tape.

I have a box of it. You're welcome to some if you want.

> *There is a rather. Long. Pause.*
>
> *Broken by GIBSON.*

GIBSON: *(Creepy voice.)* O I'll stay away alright. I'll stay away… *forever.*

> *Ghastly moment. JENNY has pulled out her gun. GIBSON sees it. They lock eyes for an instant, and then he realizes what's happened.*

GIBSON: That's the line. It's: Oh I'll stay away from your son/ alright

MATT: *(Relief.)* Oh

GIBSON: Stay away *forever.*

> *Laughter.*

MARIA: *(The line.)* Oh

MATT: *Yes.* Yes. Yeah it's, I knew it was –

MARIA: *(To JENNY.)* Thank God, right?

JENNY: I was going to blow you away, I swear to God.

"I'll stay away forever"

MATT: *(Piecing it together in his head.)* Right. Right

SAM: They're in the movie theater

GIBSON: Marge says: you're an awful man – this is after he turns around and they, they're gasping and Bart says/ it's you

MATT: *(Simultaneously.)* It's you

GIBSON: You're the one whose been trying to kill me and Marge says: you're an awful man, stay away from my son and he says: Oh I'll stay away from your son alright. I'll stay away… *Forever.*

MATT: *Yes. Yes.*

GIBSON: Which freaks Homer out.

MATT: *(Laughter, thigh slapping.)* Yes.

GIBSON: And then Sideshow Bob says oh no, sorry, sorry, that's no good, and he's frustrated, and he walks off.

JENNY: Awesome.

MATT: Yes. That is it.

MARIA: *(To GIBSON.)* That's great. That's so great.

JENNY: Can you do that with the rest of the episode?

MARIA: Oh *yes.*

GIBSON: I can't I can't I really wish I could.

JENNY: No you underestimate yourself, that was brilliant.

MARIA: That was so good.

GIBSON: I've actually never watched an episode of *The Simpsons.* That bit comes from an ex-girlfriend, she was a *Simpsons fiend,* she used to have this thing this little routine – like you'd say listen would you mind not…drumming your fingers like that and she'd say oh I'll stop drumming my fingers alright, I'll stop drumming them *forever.*

JENNY: Huh

GIBSON: Completely annoying. She's the one you really need, seriously, she knows all of them, she was always quoting from them.

> *There's that bit of a pause again.*

MATT: I'm Matt by the way.

GIBSON: Gibson.

JENNY: Jenny.

MARIA: Maria.

SAM: Sam.

> *MARIA is looking off into the woods to see if she can see COLLEEN.*

GIBSON: You were in the middle of the episode.

MATT: We were. We were in the middle, of the episode…

JENNY: Where were we?

GIBSON: Pandas.

MATT: Pandas, right. The Pandas.

MARIA: And Moe was shoeing them away 'andele andele'

JENNY: That was so much earlier we were actually

SAM: Movie theater.

MARIA: Right we were in the movie theater

MATT: I'll stay away from your son alright, I'll stay away *Forever.*

MARIA: So good.

JENNY: And then he goes off

MATT: He goes off and then next…

JENNY: They're on a houseboat, right? On –

MATT: They're on a houseboat.

JENNY: On, is it Cape Fear? In the cartoon?

MATT: Terror Lake.

JENNY: Right! And there are piranhas.

MATT: There are *piranhas.*

JENNY: And he's running, right? From the piranhas? He's running and…

MATT: Yes…yes…he *is* running – okay yes Sideshow Bob gets on the boat, and he cuts the line – and he's going to – um – he's got a machete and…

JENNY: Oh

MATT: So he takes Bart, he takes Bart out of the hold, onto the deck, and Bart like *(Finds it.) runs away* and he runs to like the back deck and he looks over the railing and there are *crocodiles*

JENNY: Oh *right*, the crocodiles.

MATT: And the crocodiles are snapping up at him and Bart says: *(Intake of breath, and then.)* 'oh no!' and so he runs to the front of the boat and there are piranhas and he says: *(Intake of breath, and then.)* 'oh no!' and he runs to the back again and there's all these crocodiles and he's like: *(Intake of breath, and then.)* 'oh…right.'

  They all laugh at this.

JENNY: But wait we're forgetting…I think there's a cactus… before…

MATT: The *road trip*. When they're driving to Terror Lake –

MARIA: *(She remembers this one!)* They drive – they drive through a cactus patch! They drive through a cactus patch! Right?!

MATT: Right, right right right! Homer's like: "hey everybody – want to drive through that cactus patch?" and they're like: "yay!" While Sideshow Bob is hanging on underneath the car: "Ouch! Ouch! Ouch!"

  The three of them laugh merrily, MATT most of all.

That's right, they drive through a cactus field singing Gilbert and Sullivan "three little something something school girls we!" "Three Little Maids from School are we! Something something something something! They're singing Gilbert and Sullivan

JENNY: Because, yes, at the *end*

MATT: Because at the end, at the very end, Sideshow Bob performs *HMS Pinafore.* The entire, the entire Gilbert and Sullivan opera.

JENNY: and at some point, at some point him and Bart are doing a duet together.

MARIA: *(She's getting a very dim transmission.)* "nope never…"

  (Half sung.) "nope never never never…"

MATT: Yeah, it's like:

MARIA: "No never?'

MATT: Yeah, "no never" and Bart's like "what never?" "What no never?" "no never!" "no never?" "no never!" and he's like, uh, *(Singing.)* sailors never never never get sick at sea!

GIBSON: *(Sung: casual, but firm.)* I'm never, never sick at sea! "What, never?" "No, never!" "What, never?"

"Well, Hardly ever!"

"He's hardly ever sick at sea!"

MATT: Aha! *Yes.*

MARIA: Nice.

MATT: An aficionado eh?

GIBSON: Worse than that, I'm afraid: I belong to a small amateur society.

JENNY: Does that mean you can do School Girls?

GIBSON: I have played Pooh-Bah in *The Mikado, twice.*

MATT: Let's hear it!

GIBSON: You certain? Because the terrible truth is, you really only have to ask me once:

MARIA: Yes!

> *Let's just pause to note parenthetically that these are none of them people who, in their previous life, would have enjoyed the idea of an impromptu Gilbert & Sullivan recital.*

MATT: Hit me.

> *A tiny preparatory pause. A breath. Then, with precision:*

GIBSON: Three little maids from school are we

Pert as a school-girl well can be

Filled to the brim with girlish glee

Three little maids from school

SAM: Bring it!

GIBSON: Everything is a source of fun

He does the little orchestral bit.

Nobody's safe, for we care for none

    Ditto.

Life is a joke that's just begun

    Ditto.

Three little maids from school

    The lights have already begun to dim

    He charges into the next verse with bounce and verve.

Three little maids who, all unwary

Come from a ladies' seminary

Freed from its genius tutelary

Three little maids from school

Three little maids from school

    COLLEEN has crept back, and watches from the margin of the woods.

The Second Act

A projection: 7 Years Later

A cozy living room.

GIBSON, in an armchair, is watching a TV which is facing away from us – he is holding a remote and is switching channels; a faint flickering plays across his face.

QUINCY enters wearing an office suit, blouse, the heels, the leather purse, the earrings.

QUINCY: Ach.

GIBSON: Ach?

>> *She lets her purse drop to the ground.*

QUINCY: Such a day!

GIBSON: Yeah?

QUINCY: SUCH a day. You're just going to – sit there, you aren't going to…come to…greet me…or

>> *She's removing her earrings.*

GIBSON: That's dogs. Sometimes children.

QUINCY: Right. Children. I was thinking about that on the drive today, there was a radio program

GIBSON: Plenty of time.

COLLEEN: Jenny I can see the plug.

>> *JENNY emerges from backstage.*

JENNY: Oh I thought I *(Sees the plug.)* oh alright. Do you want to go on, or…?

COLLEEN: Gibson is that where we set the chair?

>> *GIBSON leans over, looks at the spike marks*

GIBSON: Yup.

>> *SAM has drifted out from offstage.*

SAM: That's the spot.

COLLEEN: Maybe closer.

GIBSON: You're not getting the *(He indicates light flickering on his face.)*

JENNY: Not really.

COLLEEN: Yeah. We just don't have enough candles.

SAM: I can rig it up for more easy.

COLLEEN: Not currently in the budget. Okay…

GIBSON: Richard's, I saw one of their TV scenes, you get the color also, it looks great, I got one of their guys a couple drink after and he said they have this blue – cellophane plastic, this clear blue cellophane plastic over it so

JENNY: Yeah…

GIBSON: That wrap, remember? For food.

COLLEEN: Yeah very hard to come by.

MATT: Oh!

> *They look at him.*

A mirror, right? In the back? Behind.

SAM: Right. Nice.

COLLEEN: Well worth trying.

SAM: There's one above the sink in the bathroom I can de-install.

MATT: We're gonna need to break it.

SAM: Yah.

MARIA: Colleen this should be a bigger foot motion, yes?

> *She pantomimes the stomping.*

COLLEEN: Yeah it can be huge.

MATT: As long as you retract your foot fully, each time.

COLLEEN: Yeah all the way back, all the way forward. And Matt that second blank pause can actually be that moment/ longer

MATT: Longer. I know I know. Can we

MARIA: Yeah can we just run through the FBI scene again

COLLEEN: Oh no. Absolutely not. We've got to get the commercials in gear.

MARIA: But we've *got* to work on the episode the episode is so creaky.

COLLEEN: Absolutely. Tonight. Tonight we work on the episode.

MARIA: Okay but at this moment, I feel like it's more efficient, while it's in my head –

MATT: I'd actually I'd really love to go around again with my yelp of terror. I thought of a perfection.

JENNY: And the transition sucked. We have to work on the transition anyway.

QUINCY: The transition really did suck.

COLLEEN: Jesus Hell. Alright fine.

MARIA: From the beginning? That would be so great.

COLLEEN: Fine! But we've got to get it set up in two seconds.

MARIA: Thank you.

COLLEEN: Two seconds!

As they de-assemble the living room:

JENNY: You know what has got to be more of a thing also: Sideshow Bob. The houseboat.

MARIA: Absolutely.

COLLEEN: Right. I know. Of course. Right.

JENNY: Now it's just sort of: here I am clambering up the side of this houseboat, here I am shaking my fist, ah there's thunder, now I think I'll go inside it could just be much much more, you know, a *thing*

GIBSON: I would be more than happy for it to be more of a thing

MATT: Well it's the timing. Right now, it's all over the map.

GIBSON: Well we've never really set it.

JENNY: Yeah there's a lot of opportunity there.

COLLEEN: In our copious free time. Sam did you have a chance to adjust the padding on the rakes?

SAM: Yeah it should be a more comfortable thwack now.

GIBSON: *Thank you* Sam.

COLLEEN: *Places!*

And…

> *An FBI office. An agent speaks to HOMER. Another agent lounges nearby.*

FIRST AGENT: My name is Agent Seacrest Mr. Simpson, Agent Seacrest FBI Witness Protection Program.

HOMER: Uh huh.

FIRST AGENT: Mr. Simpson your family no longer needs to fear Sideshow Bob –

HOMER: Uh huh.

FIRST AGENT: We are relocating you to a houseboat, on Terror River.

> *He yanks down on a display screen – a map of Terror River and the adjacent scary surroundings is displayed.*

HOMER: Aah!

FIRST AGENT: And you'll have a new identity.

HOMER: Woo hoo! O.J. Simpson! O.J. Simpson!

FIRST AGENT: That identity is in use. From now on, Mr. Simpson, you will be: Mr. Thompson.

HOMER: Oooh.

FIRST AGENT: Do you understand that? That's your new identity: Mr. Thompson.

HOMER: Got it.

FIRST AGENT: Homer Simpson no longer exists – you're Mr. Thompson now.

HOMER: Got it.

FIRST AGENT: Excellent. Let's just practice this a moment shall we? How are you, Mr. Thompson?

HOMER: *(Blink. Blink.)*

FIRST AGENT: Now that's you, remember. You're Mr. Thompson now.

HOMER: Right. Right. Got it.

FIRST AGENT: Good. Let's just run through that one more time.

Good Morning! Mr. Thompson. How are *you* today, *Mr. Thompson.*

HOMER: – – – – –

FIRST AGENT: So when *I* say Mr. Thompson, you respond, *as* Mr. Thompson.

HOMER: Sure.

FIRST AGENT: Certain you're clear on this?

HOMER: Piece of cake.

FIRST AGENT: Really?

HOMER: Sure thing.

FIRST AGENT: Mr. Thompson!

HOMER: *(Blank.)*

SECOND AGENT: Okay look. I'm going to call you "Mr. Thompson" and when I say "Mr. Thompson" I'm going to *press* on your foot and when *I* press on your foot and say Mr. Thompson you say *hello*, okay?

HOMER: Fire away.

SECOND AGENT: Well Hello There Mr. Thompson *(Press.)*, Mr. Thompson *(Press.)* hello *(Press.)* Mr. Thompson, *(Press.)* Mr. Thompson Hi.

> *In frustration he stamps on HOMER's feet a few times.*
>
> *HOMER leans over, speaks surreptitiously to first agent.*

HOMER: I think he's talking to you.

COLLEEN: *(Perfunctory.)* Great.

MATT: Hey, can we just –

COLLEEN: In no universe. Onto the commercial! Go go go!

> *A living room is re-assembled.*

As it is assembled the cast sings Hectic Day:

CAST: When its been a hectic day – the cars the rush your crazy boss
When all you want to say is: stop the world and let me off
When all you need is one sweet smiling face to see you through
Brush off your shoes walk through the door your home is here for you

Your home is here for you

> *An armchair on castors sails across the stage from one direction, and is grounded. A lamp is carried out considerably slower.*
>
> *GIBSON, in an armchair, is watching a TV which is facing away from us – he is holding a remote and is switching channels; a faint flickering plays across his face.*
>
> *QUINCY enters wearing an office suit, blouse, the heels, the leather purse, the earrings.*

QUINCY: Ach.

GIBSON: Ach?

> *She lets her purse drop to the ground.*

QUINCY: Such a day!

GIBSON: Yeah?

QUINCY: SUCH a day. You're just going to – sit there, you aren't going to…come to…greet me…or

> *She's removing her earrings.*

GIBSON: That's dogs. Sometimes children.

QUINCY: Right. Children. I was thinking about that on the drive today, there was a radio program

GIBSON: Plenty of time. Come on over here.

QUINCY: All the way over there? Really?

GIBSON: C'mere.

QUINCY: Hmmmm.

> *She makes a show of walking all the way over there and plopping into his lap.*

GIBSON: Better?

QUINCY: A little. You aren't going to turn the sound up ever are you.

GIBSON: It's got to prove it's worthy.

QUINCY: Do you know what I want?

GIBSON: You want me.

QUINCY: No, no not you.

GIBSON: *(Maybe there's a wee bit of fondling.)* Are you sure?

QUINCY: Positive. It's been SUCH a day do you know what I want?

GIBSON: You want a bath.

QUINCY: So badly. Traffic was nutsballs. The fluorescents at work are driving me crazy.

> *She slides off and wanders offstage.*

GIBSON: "Nutsballs"? Seriously?

QUINCY: I think I heard it on the radio? There are some youth in my office, maybe I got it from them. I kind of like it. Hang on a sec.

> *Sound of water.*

You want to know the big news? At work?

GIBSON: *(Concerned – layoffs?)* What?

QUINCY: Someone is stealing lunches out of the refrigerator

GIBSON: Someone is what?

QUINCY: Stealing lunches! From the refrigerator!

> *She returns in a bathrobe. Maybe there is a bit of leg.*

That's low, right?

GIBSON: Very low. Lunches which are properly marked.

QUINCY: Yes. With a sharpie. In big *(Gesture.)* lettering.

Last Friday they took Raul's leftover Chinese: sweet 'n' sour pork, pineapple fried rice. And his Fritos. Although they left behind the carrot sticks.

GIBSON: And this was all in a bag

QUINCY: He knows the moment he lifts it up before he even opens it

JENNY: With his name on it in sharpie

QUINCY: Oh fuck me. With his name on it. *(Restarting.)* Although they left behind the carrot sticks.

GIBSON: And this was all in a bag

QUINCY: With his name on it! In sharpie! He goes to get his bag lunch from the fridge and all it is is carrot sticks. He knows the moment he lifts it up before he even opens it: why is this so light. Monday Leslie's sub sandwich and Javon's take-out Indian. Tuesday Peter's Thai, Pravit's leftover tuna noodle casserole, *and* Robbie's cold pizza.

GIBSON: *(Wry.)* And you've called the cops.

QUINCY: *(Very realistic.)* Sure, but what are they going to do. They came by, wrote up an event report, questioned a few people we said we need one of your guys stationed in the breakroom they just laughed

GIBSON: Wait you aren't serious.

QUINCY: We said you aren't going to interrogate anyone? You can use the conference room. We're helpless and they don't give a damn.

> *From offstage: the sound of a breakage.*
>
> *Everyone freezes, head swivels in that direction.*
>
> *A long tense beat.*

COLLEEN: Sam?

SAM: *(From off.)* Yah.

COLLEEN: That the mirror?

> *He emerges, with a large shard of mirror.*

SAM: Sorry 'bout that folks. Towel's gone, didn't want to risk a blanket.

Do you want to keep going or shall we try this out?

COLLEEN: No no let's take a look.

SAM: I'll need to install it but just to get a sense.

> *He carefully slides the glass into the TV case. The flickering light is brighter.*

GIBSON: Nice.

COLLEEN: Gibson sit back so we can get you in position…Sam that is an improvement. A definite definite improvement.

MARIA: Hurrah Sam!

MATT: Hello.

MARIA: Hurrah Matt!

COLLEEN: Excellent. No time for joy. Gibson you were, no, Quincy.

QUINCY: I was…oh. Um: you can use the conference room. We're helpless and they don't give a damn.

> *GIBSON takes a moment to re-orient, then:*

GIBSON: *(Concluding.)* You didn't actually call the cops.

QUINCY: No but it's *tempting.* Today Stephanie's doggie bag of enchiladas goes missing along with her deli container of mango chunks and her Sprite, and Michi brought in one of those Sara Lee Coffee Cakes, for the office, you know, the delicious kind, extra cinnamony, and she took a piece, and I came in right as she was putting it out and I had a piece and so did Michael but 20 minutes later – 20 minutes later! – it was all gone which is absolutely an abnormal rate of consumption – this isn't slices, this is cubes – and so we asked around, we actually went desk to desk, and so we asked around, we actually went desk to desk, and the rest of that cake is not accounted for and then, Rachael comes into the break room, there's a fresh pot of coffee

GIBSON: Kenyan?

QUINCY: Columbian.

GIBSON: *(Absently.)* Yum

QUINCY: Uh huh and we're all standing around with our mugs and she opens the freezer and she turns around with this look, on her face, and we say what? What? And she goes:

…where's my pizza pocket?

All in one day. You know what I mean?

GIBSON: Right.

QUINCY: All in one day. Nobody can eat all of that. This isn't someone who can't be bothered to go out. They're just taking it.

GIBSON: They're taking it just to take it.

QUINCY: Right? One of us is a predator.

    A little pause.

GIBSON: Huh. So there are signs up.

QUINCY: There are very angry signs.

GIBSON: And that doesn't stop this person

QUINCY: Uh uh. Yeah I think it goads them on.

GIBSON: You don't pack a lunch.

QUINCY: No, I eat out. *(Dreamily.)* I love Prêt a Manger. Their sandwiches are so cute, they're so tidily cut and packaged. I like the roast beef with arugula and parm, I also like the turkey club sandwich, the blt; it's cold outside, snow outside, but I'm tucked into the corner of the Pret cozy as can be with my perfect compact triangle of chicken salad and a hot chocolate and all the rest of the place just, gabbling, behind me.

    The water stops, then after a moment starts up again.

Hang on, I'm going to add the bath salts, *before the tub is done filling.* And maybe some bath oil.

    She goes offstage.

Oh it's all steamy in here.

Hang on…

> *Sound of person lowering herself in bath.*

Oh… Oh… Oh…yummy.

GIBSON: *(Amused.)* Nice bath?

QUINCY: *(Dreamy.)* Really nice bath.

GIBSON: You want me to bring you a glass of Chablis?

QUINCY: Mmmmh.

> *Sound of mild splashing.*

GIBSON: Or mineral water, if you want a mineral water, with a squeeze of lemon in it, or lime. Or I could get you a grape Fanta. Or one of those Italian sodas you like. Or a cran-raspberry juice. Or a Diet Coke.

QUINCY: With ice?

GIBSON: Of course with ice. Why not with ice? The freezer is chock full of ice.

QUINCY: Sounds dreamy. I'll just have a Chablis. Or, no, a Diet Coke. No, a Chablis. God it's been a long day.

GIBSON: Sure thing.

How's the bath?

QUINCY: Delicious. Rejuvenating. I feel like a Brand New Woman.

> *A pause.*

GIBSON: *(Out front.)* Yeah?

COLLEEN: *(From back of house.)* Yeah. *(Beat.)* Yeah. That's effective.

> *QUINCY emerges from backstage.*

QUINCY: It's good, right?

GIBSON: Yeah nice work, Jenny.

COLLEEN: It works.

JENNY: It's that fine line between tantalization and torture.

GIBSON: Why Chablis? Do we really have to be those kind of people?

JENNY: People respond well to Chablis.

GIBSON: I think people are forgetting the taste. And the ethos. They've reverted to pure sound pleasure: Chablis.

COLLEEN: It's an innocent wine. People like the innocence.

MARIA: Also, isn't Chablis one of those wines which was out of fashion but actually it's quite good?

GIBSON: No. Common misconception but, no. Quincy, really, do you want to be a Chablis drinker?

QUINCY: Seriously Gibson? At this point, all I care about my imaginary alcohol, is that it is aged.

COLLEEN: Gibson *I* was a Chablis drinker. Like many people, a proud proud Chablis drinker. *(Calling offstage.)* Hey what was up with the water?

MATT: *(From backstage.)* Sorry. Sorry. My bad.

COLLEEN: Do you need more water back there?

MATT: *(Coming onstage.)* I misarranged my buckets. I have a system. *(To QUINCY.)* Sorry babe.

> *QUINCY shrugs.*

MARIA: Call the plumber!

GIBSON: What about Shiraz. That sounds fun too: Shiiiraaaaz!

JENNY: Shiraz makes a lot of people slightly nervous because they don't remember if they drank it or not and if they liked it or not or even if it was red or white. The point of a Commercial is to create a reality which is *welcoming*, not challenging.

GIBSON: Yeah but what about that whole, I feel like we're failing to exploit, you know, in commercials, it's not just about feeling cozy, and bounty, there was that whole other thing commercials used to do, like, there always used to be that question of identity. Like, it's not just what is the desire, it's *who has* the desire. I think people are ready for Status again.

JENNY: You're joking.

GIBSON: In baby steps. I think people are ready for Status.

JENNY: *(Turning ever so slightly away.)* Do you know what would be great, if we could get that *smell.* That bath salt *smell.*

QUINCY: Oh I hate that smell.

JENNY: If we melted some and heated them up in a pan?

QUINCY: We'll be stuck with that smell all night.

JENNY: If we just get a hit of it at the beginning.

QUINCY: I hate that smell. I'm not alone. Sam, you hate that bath salt smell, right?

SAM: What?

QUINCY: That bath salt smell, when the tub is filling with bath salts.

SAM: Are we doing that smell?

MATT: Wait, what? Because there's a lot going on back there already.

QUINCY: Baths salts, bubble bath, that chemical odor.

SAM: I like that smell.

MARIA: Where *are* the Diet Cokes? Does anyone know?

JENNY: I heard someone trucked them all to Denver.

COLLEEN: *(From backstage.)* Do *not* relax. We'll have this resolved in a tick.

MARIA: I heard that too but that's a crazy rumor, right?

SAM: There's definitely a lot of trucking going on to Denver.

MARIA: But *all* of the Diet Cokes? There must have been so many Diet Cokes in circulation. Millions. I know a guy in Dayton who has a stash of Diet Cokes and do you know what he's selling them for? Lithium batteries. 2 a can. That's nuts. Can you imagine? I'd wait until winter and then I'd have it over ice. That *pop* sound, the sparkly fizz. "ahhhh".

GIBSON: Well if you figure. If you figure:

MARIA: Oh no.

GIBSON: If you figure population 300 million. Let's say half of that is women. 50 million. Let's say of that, like, 30 million are under 10. So that's 120 million…which is hard, let's say 50 million are under 10 or over 70 leaving 100 million women and let's pretend only *half* of them drink Diet Coke, 50 million, and let's pretend that they only have 2 a week 100 million and let's pretend that there's only 2 weeks' worth in circulation so there should be at any given Before moment 200 million Diet Cokes around in shops and warehouses and then there's an After population of a million tops

JENNY: Less than that.

MATT: No one knows.

JENNY: It has to have been far less than that, just, percentagewise.

MARIA: It's not evenly distributed.

JENNY: And we lose half again as many afterwards. Those first few years. Half again as many.

MARIA: No.

JENNY: If not more.

MATT: No one knows.

GIBSON: Let's say a million just to say and let's say half of which is women let's say a half million so for each remaining woman 400 Diet Cokes which is

QUINCY: Which actually isn't

JENNY: Over 7 years.

GIBSON: that's –

SAM: Figure half of them went up in the fires anyway.

MARIA: I was drinking a lot of them. I had them in the stream behind my place. It was hot. That summer.

QUINCY: And a lot of women aren't drinking them at all.

SAM: Men are drinking them too though. Men like the Diet Coke too.

JENNY: Gay men.

SAM: Now hey there.

JENNY: It's just a fact that gay men drink *more* diet coke than straight men.

GIBSON: Two thousand one hundred something…

MATT: My uncle the big fat butcher, *guzzled* diet coke. By the 2-liter.

JENNY: Your uncle the big fat *gay* butcher.

MATT: *Oh*. Lame.

GIBSON: Every 7 days. More or less, so. Once a week.

MARIA: I drank way more than that, when I could get hold of them. But I haven't had one for…3 years?

JENNY: Everyone was drinking it at first because of the water. People were going through soda whatever it was.

GIBSON: So actually that's, yeah. That's not so much.

MATT: So they might just be gone.

MARIA: They might just be gone.

QUINCY: Except for the guy in Dayton.

JENNY: And a stash in Denver.

COLLEEN: Assuming that any of these numbers are even vaguely meaningful.

GIBSON: Right.

COLLEEN: All right we're going to move on to Chart Hits. Hey Gib, the candles.

GIBSON: Oh right, right, sorry.

> *He leans over and blows carefully into the TV, the light diminishes, extinguishes.*

QUINCY: You know it's just as well because that stuff was going to kill you.

MARIA: No no no.

QUINCY: Don't worry I'm not going to lecture anybody, it's gone now, but that was a very scary sweetener.

GIBSON: Hey can we go a little easier on the steam?

MATT: It's a bit much?

COLLEEN: Yeah how much are you using?

MATT: That was half a stick. But the eraser is still loaded, it's good for a few more sessions.

GIBSON: It takes me back to my substitute teacher days.

COLLEEN: Go easy on it. We've only got 6 boxes and there's a fire in Heretic Homer.

GIBSON: Wait, Heretic Homer, we don't really want Heretic Homer do we?

COLLEEN: We're negotiating for it.

QUINCY: We're negotiating for it? With Primetime Players?

MATT: Not with Primetime Players with/ The Reruns

MARIA: Reruns

QUINCY: No no, I know, the Reruns, when was that decided?

GIBSON: Wait that wasn't what we decided. Heretic Homer is a wildly inaccurate show.

COLLEEN: No, we did –

JENNY: We did, Gibson.

COLLEEN: you [Quincy] were at the Landing and what you [Gibson] don't remember –

QUINCY: Alright wait yes. Yes. We can't –

GIBSON: What don't I remember? I was there.

QUINCY: Okay obviously we can't decide every decision by quorum, but I think we should decide on a *category* of decision which is decided by quorum. And I think repertoire should fall within that category of decision.

COLLEEN: *(To QUINCY. Perfunctory.)* Right. Yes. Right. *(To GIBSON.)* What you don't remember is that yes, we all agreed that Heretic Homer is a shitty show, but, a) we may be able to improve it. Matt has a line.

GIBSON: A *line*

COLLEEN: and b) Springfield Files is an even shittier show

GIBSON: But Springfield Files was a great show. People remember loving that episode.

COLLEEN: Back in the day. Yes. Our version sucks you know it does. If we don't play it we lose right to it anyway and every single time we *do* play it we diminish our reputation.

GIBSON: If we trade it we don't have a single show in our repertoire with Mr. Burns, which, this is not about me playing him it's the character, they really love him, *someone* is going to remember, someone is going to come forward.

COLLEEN: Yes. Obviously. Eventually. Look Gib, we went through all this, we decided.

JENNY: We/ did

GIBSON: We decided

JENNY: we did. We had to make a decision on it they were going to offer Heretic to Richard's.

GIBSON: We decided.

MARIA: Yes.

GIBSON: Was I peeing? I don't remember this.

COLLEEN: You were in the room.

GIBSON: Was I drinking? I. Don't. *Remember.* This.

JENNY: I think you were angry. Maybe you weren't listening.

GIBSON: Yeah but was I

MARIA: You were drinking, maybe you were drunk. [Well all right:] We were all drunk.

> *Moment while he processes this.*

GIBSON: I don't. I really don't.

Do you know what this is, do you know what this is, this is brain damage.

MARIA: Oh, no. Don't go there.

GIBSON: Of course it is. Deposits. Ruptures. Plumes. Seepage.

MATT: Gibson./ No. Really.

SAM: Gib.

JENNY: Gibson we're not going there.

GIBSON: *We don't even know* North Carolina every time it rains

MATT: Gibson put a *lid* on it.

MARIA: Gibson, please.

GIBSON: *(Continues over him.)* West Vermont – no one knows what happened to those people *no one knows what caused that* hundreds of miles from anything everything a-okay then skin peeling off

MATT: Okay. No.

GIBSON: …no-go-zones marked off with blocks of spray painted concrete and…electrical tape…that doesn't mean anything no one knows what's really going on tanks and underground everyone's guessing /no one knows the boundaries or what's creeping and what's in the water or what's we don't even know what's been seeping all this time from wherever through shale or any or

COLLEEN: Yeah…okay…

JENNY: Gibson!

QUINCY: /No. Gibson. Jesus.   MARIA: Gibson please. Please
                                          please please

GIBSON: We're breathing, we're drinking, we're eating, *it's all broken open, you know it has.*

COLLEEN: Shut up. Gibson. Shut up.

QUINCY: /No. Gibson. Jesus.

MATT: Really. Really.

SAM: Gibson.

> *SAM clasps GIBSON hard, then clamps his hands on GIBSON's skull, touches his forehead to GIBSON's. It's a half embrace, half restraint, GIBSON might be sobbing, doesn't have to be, SAM might touch his forehead to GIBSON's, it's an unusual social interaction, like something we haven't quite seen before, half comforting, half hostile, weirdly intimate,*

not sexual; what makes it unusual is that everyone else seems to take it for granted and isn't uncomfortable.

SAM: We're not going to talk about that.

There is a small recombobulating pause.

GIBSON: It's just that, I don't remember us coming to a decision. I remember the discussion. I remember... chiming in. I don't remember any moment when it was settled. It really was settled?

COLLEEN: Yes.

GIBSON: I don't remember that.

Pause.

JENNY: I think you were angry, I think you were drinking, I think you weren't listening.

GIBSON: Yeah but.

SAM: You were drinking. It wasn't a great batch, either.

MARIA: It was my batch. I'm gonna own up. It was terrible. I had a headache the whole next day.

COLLEEN: *(To GIBSON.)* Right?

GIBSON: Right.

Right.

COLLEEN: Okay?

GIBSON: Right.

A pause.

What was the line?

It takes MATT a moment.

MATT: It's a good one:

"and what if we've picked the wrong religion? Every week we're just making God madder and madder"

GIBSON: Yeah, that's good. That's a great line. The Reruns don't have that right?

MATT: Right.

GIBSON: But that's it? Just one line.

JENNY: We decided, Gibson. We really did.

MATT: People are going to bring other lines forward. That's one people remember.

GIBSON: They didn't for them.

COLLEEN: We've got a better circuit, I really think we do. If the lines are out there, they will come to us. I have every faith.

GIBSON: Jenny. Shall we discuss the booth?

JENNY and MARIA glance at each other.

JENNY: Gibson that was a private conversation.

GIBSON: I never pretended to be anything but lying there with my eyes closed resting. If anyone had bothered to say: Gibson: are you awake: I would have said 'yes'.

MATT: *What* about the booth.

COLLEEN: Jenny?

JENNY: This is something which I *(Glance at Gibson.)* have *not* brought to the attention of the group because it's serious and I'm not positive

MARIA: But you're pretty positive

JENNY: But I'm pretty positive that I don't know how much longer we can go on buying lines.

QUINCY: MATT:
What, really??   Jenny, that's. No.

COLLEEN: That's not on the table. We rely on the booth.

JENNY: You aren't dealing with people. People are making anything up and when I tell them no, thanks, it's starting to get ugly.

COLLEEN: But you've had that. People making things up, people getting angry.

SAM: You get that all the time.

JENNY: I've gotten people who are hungry, and desperate. I've gotten people who are crazy. But after the show yesterday a man came up to me, I do remember him vaguely, and he said you used my line. I said no…he said you used my line and you never paid me for it I said I can assure you, no, he said "Calm thyself, Bartron, and tell us now where the magic space crystals which can save the galaxy are hidden" I gave you that line, you said you didn't want it, and now you're using it, pay up. I said that can't have been the line you offered me.

I said look – we found the day, we found the line I wrote down – I said look, that's the line, that's your signature, that's not the line in the show

He said what is this book, what is it, it's pen on paper that doesn't mean anything, you rewrote the page, you forged my signature, you stole my line and I want my payment. And he knew, he knew it wasn't his line, he was lying to my face and he knew I knew he was lying.

This guy was bold. Lately people are bold, and that's new.

MATT: But we can't, not, if we if we stop buying lines, then we're going to lose out to shows which keep buying lines –

GIBSON: What if we restricted it just, to brokers, to people we have trusted relationships with.

MATT: But those guys…I don't know about those guys… they say they haven't got anything, you trade a show to Richards, suddenly they just 'happen' to have an entire scene. The best lines we get we get from people we don't know. People who walk right up to the booth.

MARIA: I got that person who wrote for *Saturday Night Live.*

QUINCY: Oh I remember that.

MATT: Yeah it was good, we bought it right?

MARIA: It was that whole chunk of Heart of Bartness plus some lines for Lisa the Vegetarian. And he said he had a really good piece of Much Apu About Nothing but he was the one, he said he'd have to join up, he said we'd have to take him with us.

I don't know what happened to him. Maybe he went to Richard's.

GIBSON: They're not taking people on now are they?

JENNY: Sometimes. They're also kicking people out.

MATT: Pond Creek. Pond Creek has never been great, right? We take Pond Creek off the route. Maybe we add Sulphur and Helena before we cross into Kansas. I know that's not great business, and it sucks for the horses, but they'd love to have us.

JENNY: It's not just Pond Creek. Muskogee has always been cool but two weeks ago.

GIBSON: *(Automatically.)* 3 weeks ago.

JENNY: *(With a dismissive gesture.)* 3 weeks ago. I didn't like the feeling.

MARIA: Right.

MATT: Look our episodes are getting pretty good, we're putting together a rather accurate show.

QUINCY: Richard's is having the same problem too, I bet.

JENNY: Maybe their security detail is better than ours.

SAM: Right here sweetheart.

JENNY: Honey you do a great job but you're just hiring people town to town, Richard's has 6 guys on permanently.

GIBSON: Richard's can only be in one place at a time. We don't have to be Richard's. We don't need 23 shows.

MATT: They've got 27 now.

   That's news.

MARIA: 27? Whose did they buy?

COLLEEN: Thursday Night.

MARIA: *(This is a bummer.)* Oh

JENNY: Those guys were losers anyway.

GIBSON: We don't need 27 shows. There's room for more than Richard's Couch.

COLLEEN: Let's not kid ourselves.

If Richard's has a strong enough security detail, they keep buying lines.

They keep buying lines they assemble superior shows.

Our shows look shitty in comparison. We lose audience. We lose more audience. Until we're selling our repertoire to Richard's show by show by show.

Thursday Night held out as long as they could. I think a lot of those guys went into the Shakespeares and some of them just straight out sold themselves.

There's a kind of a pause.

QUINCY: I hear Richard's has a stash of lithiums, and ten of those super powerful camping flashlights, and they're going to do a dusk to dark showing of A Streetcar Named Marge, with a spotlight finale at the end.

A bit of a pause.

JENNY: They can't keep that up for long.

MARIA: Long enough though, right?

MATT: It still kills me they've got Streetcar.

A pause.

QUINCY: Our Commercials are excellent.

MARIA: Our commercials are *great.*

COLLEEN: They *are* great. They *are* excellent. We don't need the booth, for the commercials. Alright. Alright. Keeping it together. Moving on. We've only got a few more hours of daylight and we have yet to run Chart Hits all the way through.

MATT: Chart Hits: *(Random 'Mexican' accent.)* Let's do eet!

MARIA: Chart hits!

COLLEEN: Sam, Matt, you got the car?

SAM: Rock 'n' Roll!

MATT: Booyah!

JENNY: *(On the fly.)* Costumes no costumes?

COLLEEN: Absolutely costumes

QUINCY: *(Startled.)* Goodness

JENNY: Costumes/ it shall be.

GIBSON: Has anyone seen my glasses? *(Finds them.)* Oh.

> *As people are getting into position:*

MARIA: Wait but wait, is Toxic in or out what did we decide?

COLLEEN: In for the moment.

MARIA: In.

GIBSON: It's a piece of music which does not play well with others

COLLEEN: But I want it

GIBSON: But she wants it, so it's in for another go around.

> *They get in position for the commercial, perhaps wheeling the front half of an actual convertible onto the stage.*

GIBSON: 1 2 3 4

MEN: Bum bum bum bum Bum bum bum bum

WOMEN: Zoom Zoom Zoom!

COLLEEN/SAM: Driving through the American West!

WOMEN: Zoom Zoom Zoom!

MARIA/GIBSON: Driving through the American East!

> *Somewhere in here GIBSON realizes he still has a handgun somewhere on his person and he breaks hastily from the formation to place it by the side of the stage and then returns.*

WOMEN: Zoom Zoom Zoom!

QUINCY/MATT: Driving through the American South,

MARIA/JENNY/GIBSON: South West

COLLEEN/SAM/MATT: South East

MEN: Across the Plains

WOMEN: Along the Coasts

MEN: Straddling the Borders –

ALL: with the radio ON!

SAM: Pump up the volume!

ALL: Pump up the volume!

MANY: Crank up the tuuuuuuunes!

> *What follows is a medley of popular hits from the last 10 years – generally these are not sung in solo, but arranged for best group singing effect, there is bravura dancing during this, and costume changes – the ladies, in particular, should be changing into a variety of perhaps worrisomely sexy outfits – the overall effect should be highly choreographed, polished, entertaining, and without irony. The really characteristic instrumentations of these songs should be rendered as well, but vocally.*
>
> *It includes:*
>
> *Thunder and lightening sounds.*
>
> *Heavy rain.*

and I park the car but   (and I'm parking the car)
I don't put on the brake and
you zip up your jacket and
my fingers start to shake

Because when you close that door when
You walk away it's
The end of everything between us my
new life will start today

(this is the part
Where we say
Goodbye)

Yes now I know
That I've got
to say
goodbye

(To everything we are
It's the end of everything)

And I keep my cool
And I do not cry

(It's the end of everything
Yes it's the end of everything)

And you close the door and
I drive away and
I keep my hands steady
I didn't ask you to stay

now I'm on the highway and
I roll the top down
Storm lashes my face
As I speed from this town

I'm wet with the rain
I'm all drenched with tears
My body's been shaking
For what feels like a hundred years

This is the part
where I say
Goodbye

(To everything it's
The end of everything

Yes I know that
I've got to say goodbye)

(To everything it's
the end of everything)

ending with:

ALL: The

ALL: Thomp –

ALL: sons!

Duh Duh Duh Duh Duh Duh Duh Duh – Duh Duh Duh Dah!

> *The SIMPSON's family is now in the car, HOMER is driving, he has a Witness Protection hat.*

MARGE/JENNY: It's Cape Terror kids, our new home!

And that was not enough time for the quickchange. Obviously.

> *Obviously. As she is half Marge and half showgirl.*

It's the wig, do I need to be in the last number?

COLLEEN: You do…

JENNY: Can this thing just be plopped? *(To MARIA.)* if you can get the housecoat…

MARIA: Right, and so just [before]

JENNY: Yeah, because it's just. It's a hand issue. I don't have enough hands.

COLLEEN: Okay so you can be her wig hands, everyone else?

SAM: *(BART is missing a piece.)* Me, but that's just because I zagged, when I should have been zigging. I have enough time.

QUINCY: Yeah I'm fine.

COLLEEN: Gib?

GIBSON: *(From beneath the car.)* Yeah?

COLLEEN: You had enough time to get under there?

GIBSON: Yeah, did anyone see me?

COLLEEN: I wasn't looking. I'll keep an eye on it next time.

> *There is a thunk. GIBSON crawls out from beneath the car, he is in full Sideshow Bob gear.*

GIBSON: Hey, what if he has engine oil, on his face. Just a big blot of engine oil.

JENNY: Yeah.

GIBSON: Like on the nose and *(Gesturing.)* over.

SAM: On the eye area, like a black eye

QUINCY: Like one of those dogs.

COLLEEN: If you can get it [on in time] –

GIBSON: There's time. We could use I don't know what.

COLLEEN: Was that your thunk? Coming down? That wasn't your thunk.

GIBSON: That was my thunk.

COLLEEN: There's got to be more of a thunk.

GIBSON: I don't know how much more of a thunk I can with my bare body.

COLLEEN: If there's a board underneath it maybe

MATT: Or a sheet of metal. No.

SAM: A hollow board? A piece of one of those doors.

MATT: Yeah but when [are we going to get that under there].

SAM: You know I think I saw some. In a stash of lumber in the back.

He goes in search.

MATT: This is a whole other moving part. I just want to register that.

COLLEEN: It has to be a thing, that moment, it has to be more of a thing.

GIBSON: So what do you think blot here, blot there.

COLLEEN: Yeah that could be kind of great.

MARIA: You need something black but with that reddish sheen, like, viscous but also

QUINCY: But it's a cartoon I think even just, mud, something black and solid.

MARIA: But it can't look like mud it's got to look like engine oil. So it's not just that he's dirty but it's that thing like, all during the journey, he's *clinging* to the underbelly of the car, hot engine oil, in his face uh but he holds on, he perseveres. Like that's what makes him scary.

QUINCY: I just think, something on a person's face is funny. I think it's better if it's not realistic I think that's just distracting.

COLLEEN: Okay this is that discussion.

QUINCY: This is a cartoon. That's what we're doing. A cartoon. You keep trying to turn it into a Drama.

MARIA: I'm not trying to turn it into a Drama Quincy I'm trying to create a…richer sense of reality and that's part of what makes it funny; things are funniest when they're true. *(To everyone.)* Right?

> *She gets no playback.*

QUINCY: I just think, if we're giving everything motivations, then where's the power, where's the joy. No motivation, no consequence, that's the *point* of a cartoon. Where else do we get to experience that, *nowhere.*

MARIA: I'm just saying I think we have a chance to like, to like, engage at the same time with, like…larger…are we just entertaining them? We have an opportunity here to provide…*meaning.*

QUINCY: Things aren't funny when they're true they're awful. Meaning is everywhere. We get *Meaning* for free, whether we like it or not. Meaningless Entertainment, on the other hand, is actually really hard. Look if you don't like what we're trying to do why don't you go somewhere commensurate with your matchless aesthetic. Go to one of the Dramas. I heard that blonde in *The West Wing*, the one on the Louisville circuit, is pretty sick. Maybe they'll take you in there.

> *Beat.*

GIBSON: Quincy. Jesus Christ.

COLLEEN: *(Stand down.)* Maria.

> *A moment of eye contact, then MARIA walks off.*

MATT: Babe.

QUINCY: What?

SAM: I think I got it

COLLEEN: Alright we're going to keep it moving. Gib, can you get back in there? Under.

Gib.

GIBSON: *(After the tiniest moment.)* Yes. Yeah. Right on it.

COLLEEN: Sideshow Bob, everyone. Sideshow Bob, ah, emerging.

SAM: Let me just slide this.

> *GIBSON knocks on it.*

COLLEEN: And are the rakes in position?

JENNY: Yup.

> *The others move backstage.*
>
> *GIBSON gets into position then*
>
> *with an audible* thunk

COLLEEN: Excellent. I heard that.

> *Sideshow Bob detaches himself from the chassis, and creeps out from under the car*
>
> *(accompanied by creepy music)*
>
> *he stands, he is lit from behind, creepy music, low thunder from the horizon, a flash of lightning*
>
> *he steps forward, raising his hand to shake his fist.*

JENNY/COLLEEN/QUINCY: Wah Wah Wah Wah
Wah Wah Wah Wah
Wa Wa Wa

GIBSON: At last, Bart Simpson, at last! While you and your family cozy yourselves away in this houseboat; while you play cards, while you drink hot cocoa, I shall be lurking here, on the river bank, like a crocodile – only with much better skin, and a superlative singing voice – and come nightfall –

> *He steps forward, raising his hand to shake his fist...*
>
> *(Alas, although he does not see it, he is just about to step on a rake.)*

> *And then is distracted by something at the back of the auditorium.*

Show's not 'til tomorrow gentlemen.

> *COLLEEN turns and faces the audience, speaking to someone at the back of the auditorium.*

COLLEEN: *(Sharp, an edge.)* What's going on here?

GIBSON: It's fine, Colleen, it's fine – *(Out.)* something we can help you with?

> *MATT has emerged on one side, JENNY and QUINCY on the other.*

COLLEEN: *(Totally 100% combative.)* If you don't have any business here, which you do not, I strongly suggest, gentlemen, that you turn yourselves around

MATT: Colleen/ shut it.

JENNY: Colleen!

COLLEEN: march yourselves back through that door, [and return tomorrow afternoon].

> *JENNY and MATT have moved forward.*
>
> *The sound, from the back of the house, of weapons being taken off safeties.*

Motherfuckers

> *She bends down and pulls out a sidearm taped to her leg (or in some other maybe more practical way concealed on her person).*
>
> *JENNY and MATT vault forward, along with GIBSON, to restrain her.*

GIBSON: I think you'll find –

COLLEEN: Motherfuckers!!!

> *GIBSON clamps his hand over her mouth.*

GIBSON: I think you'll find pretty much anything which would be of interest in the back of our wagon. Maria? Maria?

> *MARIA has emerged from backstage, stands half on half off.*

You have the key, right?

MARIA: *(Half-frozen, half a whisper.)* Yes.

GIBSON: Can you just bring it out?

> *She turns to go. A shot rings out from the back. MARIA falls.*
>
> *Chaos:*
>
> *SAM appears from the back with a rifle.*
>
> *MATT ducks backstage.*
>
> *QUINCY grabs COLLEEN to drag her offstage though she's still grappling with her gun.*
>
> *VERY ABRUPT BLACKOUT.*

The Third Act

75 years later.

Ranged across the stage: a chorus of the citizens of Springfield.

Their faces bear a blurred similarity to faces we may recall from the TVseries: Chief Wiggham, Nelson, Principle Skinner, Apu.

Edna Krabappel leads them.

Thunder.

CHORUS OF THE SHADES OF SPRINGFIELD

There is a humming, and a musical set of syllables and sounds.

They create a highly musicalized version of an ambulance siren, then a version of a civil alert siren

Meanwhile some musical urgent something underneath

Meanwhile there is a choreography, and a dance.

CHORUS: The call came on the radio
   and then the siren blared
   And one by one all over Springfield
   lights in windows flared

       The urgent something is foregrounded, intensifies, changes.

CHORUS: The call came on the radio
   Chief Piggum grabbed his cap
   Apu said use these buckets

APU: There will be no charge for that

     CHORUS PLUS APU.

   And Willy grasped his rake.

WILLY: I shook it with a mighty curse

CHORUS PLUS APU & WILLY:
   Ms Krabappel grabbed her bullhorn,
   and Thelma grabbed her purse
   Ned Flanders seized his cross

FLANDERS: Because God is always handy

> *CHORUS PLUS APU & WILLY & FLANDERS.*

And now that Apu's back was turned Nelson

ALL: grabbed the candy

NELSON: *(A half rap.)*
Yes I grabbed the candy and I jammed it in my mouth
And I ran whooping to the yelling and the crowd was
moving south that crowd was surging to the end of town
where walls of flame rose through the air

ALL: And we all ran over there

We ran towards the sirens blare.

CHORUS: The smoke is streaming through the night

ALL: and through the night a glare

TROY MCLURE: *(Spoken.)*
Good evening, I'm Troy McClure, you may know me.

ALL: We heard a boom was there a bomb

Mayor Quimby raised his hands for calm.

Moe passed round pitchers of Chablis.

EDNA KRABAPPEL: And no one shouted flee,

ALL: Yes no one thought to flee

TROY MCLURE: *(Half-spoken.)*
Good-good-good-good evening, I'm Troy McClure

ALL: No, no one thought to flee

TROY MCLURE: *(Spoken.)* You may know me. I'm here to
report a fire, and an explosion, at the Springfield Nucyalur
[sic] Power Tower

> *Steadily, the CHORUS intones a version of the Cape Fear
> soundtrack.*

TROY MCLURE: *(Spoken.)* What's that Kent? I'm receiving
a report from the site…confirm that…power plant…Mr
Burns is *inside* the building…

NELSON: *(A rap.)* I said it's only a fire the flames were cracking like bones I turned the corner rising over our homes the tower is broke no joke broken, smokin', I can't stop lookin' and catch a whiff of that smell that's not humans cookin? I said fellahs, ladies, follow after me – there's people in there, there's employee we gotta –

ALL: Run we gotta run we gotta –

EDNA KRABAPPEL: Above the smoke there is a moon

ALL: Gotta run we gotta run we gotta

EDNA KRABAPPEL: Behind the flame a million stars

NELSON: Feets don't fail me feets don't fail me fuh-fuh-fuh feets don't fail me

(don't fail me feets!)

ALL: Survivors struggle to their cars

TROY MCLURE: Citizens are asked to remain calm and to stay where they are

ALL: The parking lot there's bodies strewn

TROY MCLURE: There is no reason to evacuate.

ONE: Krusty gasped and rubbed his eyes

ANOTHER: Principal Skinner dropped his tea

ALL: Remember

TWO: Sideshow Bob went dashing forward

ALL: Remember

THREE: That kid Martin yelped with glee

TROY MCLURE: *(Somehow distant and tinny.)* Please remain where you are. There is no danger of another explosion. There will not be a release.

NELSON: Feets don't fail me fuh-feets don't fail me fuh-feets don't fail me now! No no no no don't fail me now!

SOME: No one thought to flee

SOME: No no one knew to flee

ALL: And we just can't get there fast enough smoke whippin
through the air make me gasp and stuff where the towers
were are two pillars of light and I hear the screams in the
lit up night and I'm stopped in my tracks just like Lot's wife

TROY MCLURE: Kent? Kent? You're breaking up, Kent. Ka-ka-
ka-ka Kent?

Ka ka ka ka ka ka ka ka

ALL: The darkness blooms with a radiant bright I know in my
soul this the crazy life (upside inside out) I see you through the
smoke (-uh-) (the sky is devil red) you reach for me but I'm
broke (-uh-), (the world is made of flame) I twist and turn and
choke (-uh-) this is the vida loca, we are living the vida loca

CHORUS: The core is cracked asunder
Dark darlings are unleashed

ALL: The world is broken open
And from it spills a Beast

CHORUS: The wind is filled with hunger

ALL: Our bodies are a feast

O

Our bodies are a feast
Hee-ah Hee-ah Hee-ah Hee-ah

TROY MCLURE (WITH BACKUP): *(Half-spoken.)*
You you you you you may know me
You may have known me
Maybe you knew me
Now there's no knowing me

MORE: No one thought to flee no one knew to flee

EDNA KRABAPPEL: *(et al.)* Lisa Marie Kapner, Quentin Louis
Pease, Tavonda Ellis-Frazier, Georgia Ann Devris, Martin
McKnight Levin, Susannah Sara Quinn, Cecilia Calderon,
Michael Scott Nguyen, Huda Nizar Al-Zahawi, Jennifer
Halloway, Alberto John DiRossi, Chai Samantha Wei
Liz Owens, Bran Ostrowski, Roger Emerys, Juan Raul
Murillo Pete Aaronson, Joan Guzman, Sky Brady, Grace
Yamamoto

> *NAMES until it's a rushing overload of names each contending seriously to be heard.*

Neha Chowdhurry, Anita Brown, Muriel Friedman, Adam Dewan, Sharon Healey, Kenji Cavanaugh, Richard Djinjishashvili, Torri Law

MANY: There's just one family

MORE: There's only one family

BART: Mom! Dad! Lisa! Maggie! THIS way!

EVEN MORE: Runs towards their destiny
  On a dark and savage journey
  Runs from catastrophe
  To their final agony

ALL: The Simpsons
  The the the the the the Simpsons

> *The curtain parts: a houseboat.*

> *BART steps forward and sings:*

BART: Now I stand on the deck
  I feel the boat sway
  Bodies pass on the current
  My old life floats away

  The first drops of rain
  The first hours of night
  Our first moments of sorrow
  Our first day of flight

HOMER: I'm a brand new man
  It's a bold new day
  My family is safe
  And we're sailing away

MARGE AND LISA: But we don't know where
  We are sailing to
  And we don't know what
  We are going to do

> The rivers rage
> To the end of day
> And morning is
> So far away

HOMER: We'll sail to the horizon
> And if we fall off
> We'll pick ourselves up
> We'll dust ourselves off

MARGE: There's a storm coming,

LISA: I know I know

MARGE: There's a storm coming,

LISA: I know I know

MARGE AND LISA: There's a storm coming
> I knooooooow
> I knooooooow

HOMER: A little rain, never hurt anyone
> A little trouble makes us strong
> A noisy sky, never hurt anyone
> Marge and Lisa, Marge and Lisa…what's wrong? What's wrong?

MARGE AND LISA: If we could only return to Springfield
> Night glittered bright as day
> Lights shone on every corner
> Lamps glowed in each café
>
> The movie theater flickered
> With every story known
> And when you long for someone
> You grab the telephone
>
> The air is filled with music
> Streets are filled with laughter
> The sky is filled with stars
> You say I'll call you after

But if we had a telephone
It could only ring and ring
There's no one there to answer
Streets are filled with nothing

We want to go back to Springfield
To glide through all those days
Each crowd a pack of stories
Each heart a signal blaze

HOMER: You ladies with your fussing
Everything will be just fine
We'll play cards and drink *hot
cocoa*, have a real good time

We'll pretend there is no river
We'll pretend there is no night
We'll drop the shades ignore the storm
It will be alright
Yes it will be alright
Everything will be alright

>   *They all go inside except for BART who sings:*

BART: The sky has turned a muddy green
The river now is black
The world is filled with lightning
Oh we're never going back
I know

>   *From inside:*

HOMER: Bart!

BART: Coming Dad.

There is no going back

>   *He goes inside.*
>   *Sound of thunder*
>   *Sound of rain*
>   *Sound of thunder*

Sound of lightning.

A gloved hand, grasps the first rung of the ladder.

The cast has gathered, not in character, at the back of the stage.

Using the Cape Fear soundtrack as a base, they build an eerie soundscape:

CHORUS: Whaaa Whaaaa Whaaaa

whomp whom whomp whomp whomp whomp

Whaaaa-whaaaaa wahhh

whomp whomp whomp whomp whomp whomp

Whaaaa-whaaaaa wahhh

Another gloved hand grasps the ladder.

Grips there for a moment...

and then with a terrifying effort BURNS hauls himself up onto the deck, inch by inch, a sword clamped in his teeth.

He stands on the deck, burning with intensity. He might shake his fist. He takes it all in:

thunder

lightning

thunder

and then turns and saunters in.

From within the houseboat: screams.

CHORUS: The moon is beating on the clouds

She longs to shed her sliver light

But all the clouds are in his pay

They will not leave until the day

And day will never end this night

No day will never end this night

Scratchy, a mouse-demon, and Itchy, a cat-devil, lead the Simpsons Family onto the deck, all are bound, gagged, perhaps hooded.

Ala Three Little Maids...

ITCHY & SCRATCHY MEDLEY: Two little darling lads are we
　　Charming disarming full of glee
　　Frolicksome as such sprites can be…
　　Everyone's going to be sad

　　Nobody's safe for we care for none
　　Appalling things are a source of fun
　　Death is a joke that's just begun…
　　Everyone's going to be sad

　　　　BURNS opens the door.
　　Three little lads who all unwary
　　Worried a family – are we scary?
　　Come let us all be extra merry

BURNS: *(A low rasp, not sung.)* Everyone's going to be sad

ITCHY & SCRATCHY: Things are going to tuuuuurn out bad!

BURNS: Itchy. Scratchy – whichever one you are:

　　　　He signals I&S to remove the gag from BART.
　　Bart Simpson. After so many years.

BART: Mr. Burns. Looks like the cat dragged you in.

MR. BURNS: *You're* looking as fresh as a daisy;
　　life has been kind to you, a pity;
　　the world has so much to teach us, and
　　it's my responsibility and
　　yes I will confess it, my pleasure,
　　to see that you are educated

BART: Sucks for you I'm such a bad student

BURNS: I feel I can motivate you to learn;
　　Our first teacher is our loving family

　　　　He signals to ITCHY and SCRATCHY.

BART: *(Bluffing.)* Loving family? Ha! Homer there is
　　a small-time drunk, my sister is the most
　　annoying nerd on the planet and Mom
　　God love her, ya gotta love 'er but that
　　blue hair, the nagging, well good riddance to

them all, that's what I say, I'm better off
without them, it's time I was my own man.

BURNS: You'll be alone Bart Simpson, soon enough.

BART: *(Trying to affect a casual air.)*
The beef you have is with me Mr. Burns
why don't you just let my family go now

BURNS: Let them go you say. Let them go where? Out
into the storm? That would hardly be kind.
I slipped the rope as I plunged from the dock:
we're mid-stream now, in the middle of a
raging river; if the crocodiles don't
eat them the piranhas will and if the
piranhas won't the current will dash them
into a thousand pieces on the rocks
no, much better if we remain inside
tonight; we'll play cards, and drink *hot cocoa.*

> *BART struggles against his bonds.*

> *BART busts out singing:*

BART: M. Burns you'd better back away
You'd better toss that knife aside
'Cause you're messin' with a Simpson
A man of fury and pride!

> *Gagged, bound, HOMER grunts his approval.*

LISA: *(Singing.)* That's right you're messing with The
Simpsons!

BART: Cowabunga! Way to bust a gag, Lis!

LISA: Mind over Matter, lil'bro. Watch and learn.

> *Abruptly and with total brio they turn their heads towards*
> *BURNS and sing with defiant vigor:*

BART & LISA: That's right you're messing with The Simpsons!
We're a United Family
Yes you've provoked the wrath of Simpsons!
If you've got half a brain you'll flee.

LISA: You're gonna go from dreams of glory!
   To the gutter and the skids

BART: There's a chance you coulda done it too…

TOGETHER: If it weren't for these darn –

> *ITCHY reveals a set of Nightmare on Elm St Freddie claw-blades.*
>
> *BART and LISA stop in horror.*
>
> *BART is gagged.*

LISA: O!

BURNS: Rebel Simpsons: I've come over all chills.

LISA: Now you look here, Mr. Burns! –

> *LISA is gagged.*

BURNS: A spitfire! Ex-*cellent*. You have the same
   Antic spirit as your loveable scamp
   brother I adore a little spitfire.
   Just take a look at these wee enchanting
   fistacuffs such a fierce determined wadge
   of digits why, I could just eat them up.

> *He gnashes his teeth, delicately, and threateningly.*

   Now take a gander at these babies here –
   appetizing, no? No? You don't think so?
   Oh – I see you are distracted by my
   tattoos: well let me tell you a little
   story: the story of the left hand and
   the right hand: the story of the *world*:
   This is all, of course, enacted.
   L-O-V-E, love. Proud, triumphant, pert.
   But along comes ol' H-A-T-E hate.
   And there is a battle royale but not
   to worry Love is a winnin' Love is –
   oh but no, no, tell me it isn't so
   Love isn't a winnin' no longer Love

is a strainin' Love is a strugglin' Love
is down! Down for the count! 10! 9! 8! 7!
Is that an eyelash I see flutterin' there?
No! Love is out cold! 6! 5! O wake up
Love, wake up – Little Children, Ladies and
Gentlemen *(This is to the audience.)* we got to rouse Love in
time
We've got to make such a clappin' and a
Clatterin' and a callin' we got to
wake Love up! Wake Love up folks, wake Love up!

4! 3! O louder little children still!
Bang your hands together! 2! I see Love
Stirrin! I see Love fixin' to rise but
Will Love rise in *time*?! O shout to the roof
Ladies! Gentlemen throw your caps in the
air! And children, little children, *beat* your
hands together pound them as hard and as
fast as ever you can and yell! Yell for
Love, little children yell for Love – 1! …And…
up Love springs! Just in the nick of time and
beats ol' H-A-T-E handily!

> *The story has ended.*

Reassuring, isn't it. So you see,
Little Lisa Simpson, I bring you love,
Love triumphant, love captivating love
Intoxicating, delectable, love
just so gosh darn yummy, here, have a taste:

> *BURNS is about to slip his finger under LISA's gag as she murphs in panic.*

> *HOMER busts his gag. Brave, very optimistic:*

HOMER: *(Singing.)*

Just remember Little Lisa
Everything will be alright
Hope will always triumph

Day will always follow night

Everything will be alright

Everything will be al –

> *BURNS clamps HOMER's face. In a gesture which should recall Sam's Act 2 comforting of GIBSON.*
>
> *Time stops for a moment.*
>
> *HOMER sinks, dead, to the ground.*

SCRATCHY: *(Ala NELSON.)* Ah ha.

BURNS: You heard your daddy, pumpkin', every little thing is gonna be just fine. Now where was I? Oh that's right. I was singing:

They said I was the kind of guy who

couldn't be trusted

You said you were sure my attitude

> *He has pulled Marge towards him, as if for a dance.*

could be adjusted

> *He breaks her neck, drops the body back towards I or S.*

I told you I was wild and that someday

I would have to bust free

You said maybe you will but I know

that you'll never hurt me

Baby, there's no use

In bawling

A guy like me

Should wear a warning

I'm dangerous

You're fallin'

> *Over the course of this next verse he slowly slips his thumb into her mouth.*

ITCHY & SCRATCHY: There's no escape, I can't wait

BURNS: You need a hit babe I'll give you it

ITCHY & SCRATCHY: He's dangerous, I'm lovin' it

BURNS: Do you feel me now

ITCHY & SCRATCHY: He's toxic you're slipping under

BURNS: Just one taste of my poison paradise

ITCHY & SCRATCHY: O you love what he does tho it's so very toxic…

>*All withdraw (or are dragged) into the houseboat.*

CHORUS: When love first falls upon his knee
>His mother heals him with a kiss
>and this is how love comes to learn
>hurt is succeeded by a bliss

>But hate knows every single wound
>Leaves a scar that lasts forever
>Hate knows that every story ends
>On a dark and raging river
>Hate knows every story ends
>On a dark and raging river…

>*Song changes.*

>And now the sky is filled with stars
>The moon floats high the moon floats high
>You cannot see it for the storm
>The stars and moon are safe and warm

>the birds are shaken from the trees
>their nests are torn and blown away
>they try to rise they try to fly
>the wind fills in their wings they die
>Wings ripped apart by wind they die

>*BART screams.*

>*The door opens, and MR. BURNS, spattered with blood, pushes BART out onto the deck.*

BURNS: Your family can't help you any longer

Steady, don't even think of trying to jump
the crocodiles and piranhas will have
to wait, just until *I've* finished with you

>*Thunder, lightning, thunder.*

Now take a good last look at all of it.

Have you seen everything there is to see?

Then you'll want to make your final goodbyes

>*Thunder, lightning, thunder.*

>*BART sings.*

>*This song recalls the high point of the second act medley.*

>*As he sings, a chorus files on stage, made up of his beloved
family members, now shades, who assist in the back-up vocals
and harmonizing.*

BART: I stand on the deck and
I don't feel the boat sway
My heart's already gone my
Soul's already slipped away

This is my final hour
In the heart of a storm
No peace in my heart
Nothing warm

This is the moment
When we say
Goodbye
The whole world and I
The whole world and I
And I keep my cool
And I do not cry
I only want
to say
goodbye
To everything
It's the end of everything

The woods are ablaze
lightning cracks in the sky
smoke full of ashes and
thunder on high,

I'm wet with the rain
I'm drenched with my tears
I've been alive for
What feels like a hundred years

This is the part where I say goodbye
This is my final lullabye
Everyone I love has gone
I'll have joined them, by the dawn
Yes I'll have vanished, by the dawn

> *If a musicality has been happening (humming, crooning etc.)*
> *it ceases abruptly when BURNS speaks.*

BURNS: Wonderful! I love a poignant warble.

You may think me soft; it *is* a foible.

> *He runs a menacing finger just almost touching the surface*
> *of BART's skin.*

This has been a sweet reverie, under
A dewy sky, but the dream is over
Wakey wakey Bart Simpson: time to die

BART: *(Simple.)* Do you want me to kneel? Or stand. Or sit.

BURNS: Now is this the famous Simpsons Spirit?

It's in there somewhere – how I fear it! Boys:

> *At a snap from BURNS, ITCHY lays down a rhythm*

Although you might refuse to believe that a gentleman
with my feminine propensities my sweet sweet temper my
love of babies amenities candies is gonna mash your skull
open slide your eyeballs out of the sockets and gulp 'em
down neat I'm going to enjoy the taste of your face and
your defeat.

> *Wants a reaction.*

Nothin'? A shame. You're sadly lacking zest

Let's make this interesting:

> *He signals ITCHY & SCRATCHY and they pass him his*
> *gloves, which he puts on, and a naval saber, and they press*
> *a cutlass into Bart's hand.*

do your best

BART: However you want. Let's just get it done.

HOMER: *(Singing.)* You have to hope when hope is senseless
son

BURNS: Certain you're ready? No last minute plea?

BART: Bring it. Hit me.

> *As BURNS twirls his sword about in a teasing fashion:*

HOMER: *(Singing.)* You've got to breathe, when breath is
useless

MARGE: *(Singing.)* You've got to love when love is gone

LISA: *(Singing.)* You've got to carry on, Bart, you've got to
carry on!

> *BURNS jabs his sword straight at BART who instinctively*
> *raises his to block it.*

BURNS: Bart Simpson: trust you to bungle dying

> *BART looks at his raised sword with irritation.*

BART: That was a reflex, I wasn't trying.

LISA: *(Singing.)* You've got to keep your eyes open, when all
you can see is shit

SHADE CHORUS: *(Singing.)* Never surrender the world, never
turn from it.

> *Swiftly this time, BURNS operates his sword; again, BART*
> *blocks it, there is a brief rapid exchange of swordplay.*

BART: You just startled me – I'm raring to die!

BURNS: Dear boy, your savage pose says that's a lie.

> *BART looks down at himself, his fighting posture.*

BART: I'm going to prove myself

BURNS: *(Shouting at Chorus:)* Stop the music!

>*He throws his cutlass on the deck with a clatter.*

BART: *(To BURNS.)* This moment you own it better not let it go you've only taken two shots do not miss your chance don't blow this opportunity to end my lifetime

>*BART closes his eyes.*

Come on Bart get yourself into place face the long goodbye the final sigh sayonara suckers cold cruel world toodleoo

>*Opens his eyes.*

Burns, snap to it, let's see what you can do.

>*BURNS hands the sword to ITCHY, and begins to deglove in a slow and sinister fashion one finger at a time as:*

BURNS: *(With a bum bum bum bum varient underneath.)* I'm not going to *strain* to dispatch you there's no escape hatch for you this boat is spinning on a river in a world that's wrong your family gone the forest on fire there's no life to aspire to no air no earth that won't expire you and if you could learn to hope again to conquer dread – yes that's right, Ghost Simpsons, I'm not deaf, I've been perfectly aware of your off-key musical maunderings from the beginning –

BART: Ghost Simpsons?

BURNS: *(Continuing.)* it wouldn't Matter Little Bartlet you'd still be just as dead dead dead!

BART: *(He can't see them.)* Mom? Dad?

>*MAD CHORAL OUTBREAK.*

HOMER: Nothing protects us son, nothing holds us nothing leads us on but we tumble ahead anyway we scrape we bleed we bite you're going to fight and fight –

>*ITCHY & SCRATCHY are swept up in the enthusiasm.*

ITCHY: Fight and fight and fight and fight and fight!

BURNS: Itchy!

ITCHY & SCRATCHY remember themselves and reassume Menacing Flunky postures.

SHADE CHORUS: Fight and fight and fight and fight and fight!
Fight and fight and fight and fight and fight!

BART sings.

BART: There's no one looking after me
Just shadows and their history
There's nothing for me up ahead
The river curves and then I'm dead
But I believe that I'm going to stick around
For another second or two
Because I've never done what I've been told
And Burns you don't want me to
I believe I'm going to stick around
For another second or two
I'm going to make a little trouble

(To the family.)

Gonna cause a hullabaloo!

BART takes a fighting stance with fists raised.

This rouses great enthusiasm in the CHORUS.

BURNS throws back his head and laughs.

BURNS: Oh-ho I'm afeared now, yes, *mighty* afeared

A choral undersong rises.

Everything is now taking place in slo motion.

They both jolt suddenly, then again.

As they jostle about:

BURNS & ITCHY & SCRATCHY: Rapids!

BART & HIS FAMILY: *(And maybe CHORUS.)* Rapids!

BURNS & ITCHY & SCRATCHY: No!

BART & HIS FAMILY: *(And maybe CHORUS.)* Oh!

BURNS: Noooooooooooooooo!

They hit the rapids proper.

All are flung about.

ITCHY, is flung over the side.

SCRATCHY, is flung over the side.

BURNS' sword flies from his grasp and lands on the deck.

BART surges towards the sword, BURNS surges towards the sword.

BURNS is flung – almost over the side! But he clings to BART's leg.

BART stands above him, clutching the sword.

BURNS: This is no Victory Bart Simpson and
    don't imagine that it is you may have
    Succeeded but you haven't Triumphed, no,
    Only freakish dumb luck plucked you from me
    and if you think God or fate, fortune or
    any assortment of sentimental
    somesuch *rescued* you oh my delightful
    little charmer, what a savage surprise
    is the rest of your life going to be

BART: This is it Burns. You're never coming back.

BURNS: *(Sly, mocking.)* What, never?

BART: No, never!

BURNS: *(The same.)* What, never?

      BART drives a sword into BURNS. He registers it, although not quite as much as you'd think he would.

Kill me now Bart Simpson yes
kill me all you like but don't be surprised
when you and I meet again I'm never
leaving I don't go away I'm here for
a hundred years I'm here for a thousand
years a hundred thousand a *million* I
will be here Bart Simpson for Forever

      BURNS releases BART's leg, and slips into the river.

BART: You'll stay away Forever!

> *BART throws BURNS into the river.*
>
> *A SLOW ELECTRIC DAWN.*

CHORUS: The clouds have parted for the stars
   They're glowing stunning in the sky
   The rain has ended and the river
   Has subsided flowing softly by

   The birds are calling for the dawn
   On the horizon is first light
   And the warm wind of morning
   Will dispel this endless night
   The warm wind of the morning
   Brings the dawn and dawning light

> *BART rises, comes to stand at the railing, and slowly starts to sing:*

BART: And now that I've lost everything
   Now that everyone I love is gone
   All I have left is everything
   The river carries me on
   Though every fear is facing me

   And I do not know what next will be
   And I cannot know what next I'll see
   I'm running forward anyway
   I'm not afraid to meet the day
   The world is filled with everything
   I'm a boy who could be anything
   And now I will do everything
   The whole world unfurls before me
   A great adventure lies before me
   I'm reaching out for anything
   I'm calling out to everything
   There's nothing I'm afraid to be
   The world is new and glittery

I run to meet it hopefully
Love never dies in memory
and I will meet life gloriously

> *The rest of the cast has come out on stage during the later half of this, there are various vocal back-ups, everyone joins on the last line.*

> *As this is happening a variety of fixtures: strings of Christmas tree lights, maybe old theater lights, maybe one of those artificial candle sconces or plastic electric menorahs, table lamps, perhaps even a chandelier, or two!, hung throughout the theater, are clicking on one by one.*

> *By the end the stage is a blaze of light.*

ALL: Yes I will meet my life so gloriously
I meet life so gloriously
Yes gloriously

> *Tableau.*

> *Actors take their bows.*

> *A trap rises with the actor playing MR BURNS frantically pedaling a bicycle connected to a treadmill. As he pedals the mechanism malfunctions, and the lights slowly dim to blackness.*

> *End.*

WWW.OBERONBOOKS.COM

Follow us on www.twitter.com/@oberonbooks
& www.facebook.com/oberonbook